PROFESSIONAL PRESENTATIONS

PROFESSIONAL PRESENTATIONS

How to Succeed in International Business

Tracy Henninger-Chiang and Judee Reel

Ann Arbor
THE UNIVERSITY OF MICHIGAN PRESS

Copyright © by Tracy Henninger-Chiang and Judee Reel 1998
All rights reserved
ISBN 0-472-08447-X
Library of Congress Catalog Card No. 97-60702
Published in the United States of America by
The University of Michigan Press
Manufactured in the United States of America

2001   2000   1999   1998   4   3   2   1

Preface

When we decided to write this book, we had a vision of the type of book we would like to have for our own classes. We wanted an advanced-level presentation book that was written from a truly international perspective. Both of us have taught in and outside of the United States, and we felt that many of the presentations textbooks available were great for beginning presenters but were insufficiently challenging for the more advanced English speaker who needed to be able to make presentations professionally and in an international context. The book begins with simple exercises and activities, but it soon progresses to more difficult tasks. By the end of the book, the student is making complex and detailed presentations and working on sophisticated vocabulary and communication skills.

We have designed this book to be used in a classroom, in a self-study environment, or in a one-on-one tutoring situation. Each exercise and presentation includes instructions for both a class and a self-study student. Although you can skip around, the chapters are planned to build on one another and work most naturally in the numerical order in which they appear in the book.

The first chapter is a quick-and-easy needs analysis. (As most instructors know, a thorough needs analysis is long and much more complex.) The purpose of the needs analysis is to assist teachers and learners in identifying which skills are needed and in planning their goals accordingly. The analysis covers what the learners already know about presentations and what they need to work on, as well as reasons learners may have for needing to make presentations, now or in the future. The results of the needs analysis may be used to modify the course or self-study sessions to fit the specific needs of the learners. The more thoroughly and specifically the questions are answered, the more helpful the needs analysis will be. When written down, the results of the needs analysis can serve as a checkpoint to make sure the learner is meeting his or her goals.

The core chapters in this book include the following sections:

An Introduction to the Subject Matter. This section includes an in-depth discussion of the chapter's topic, including valuable tips and suggestions, and sometimes practical exercises that help the learner grasp the concepts, practice the skill, and prepare for the presentation.

Vocabulary and Grammar Exercises. The Word Banks contain vocabulary that will be of use to students when they talk about presenting and will also serve to increase and strengthen a high-intermediate or advanced student's vocabulary. In most cases, we have provided the learners with sample sentences so that they will know how to use the words provided. In other cases, the sentences are used within the context of the chapter.

Each Word Bank includes vocabulary exercises that reinforce the new words. We have also included usage tips under the heading, "What Your Dictionary Might Not Tell You."

In several chapters, there are grammar exercises that help learners with trouble areas. We have limited these exercises to allow instructors to prepare their own exercises based on the specific needs of their students. Those that we have included, we felt, are of a universal nature and would be of interest to most learners and instructors.

Cross-Cultural Issues. In each chapter we have included a cultural issue for learners to think about and discuss. Learners have the opportunity to examine their own culture in a way that they might not have done before. This is a unique feature of this book. The purpose is not to impose an empirical standard for giving presentations but rather to hone the individual's sense of what an effective presentation is in different cultures and in different situations and to adapt his or her presentation style to accommodate these differences.

Good and Bad Samples or Examples. We have included in most chapters an example of certain aspects of presenting that contribute to a universally good or bad presentation. Our intention is to encourage learners to examine and improve their presentation skills by identifying the good and bad elements of a presentation.

Presentation Exercises. Each of the core chapters of this text includes a presentation assignment. We know from our own teaching and learning experiences that we all learn best by doing. Learners using this book will have the opportunity to make numerous presentations. If the class time is limited, the instructor may choose to eliminate certain presentations, but we strongly encourage the instructor to include all presentations, if there is time. The majority of the presentations are short and intended to develop the specific skills covered in the chapter.

There are also short Special Presentation chapters that focus on particular situations, such as Dealing with the Media and, in an appendix, an optional longer presentation, the Hotel Project.

Observe and Give Feedback. Each core chapter also has a section for the learners to observe himself or herself, a classmate, a colleague, or an outside presenter in order to learn to recognize good presentation skills. This section also includes the opportunity to give feedback to one another about presentations. We feel that this is a fundamentally important element, and, for this reason, we offer Evaluating Presentations and Giving Feedback early in the text in chapter 2. It is essential for speakers to learn to evaluate presentations and give feedback if they are to improve their own skills as presenters.

Appendices. We encourage instructors and learners to use our special appendices as the valuable resources they are. They include contact and bibliographical information about a variety of presentation resources for business professionals. In addition, we have included an appendix on giving presentations in a variety of cultures, the information of which is based on our research and is not available elsewhere.

Contents

Chapter 1

First Steps

ASK YOURSELF!

Think about these questions and then do the exercise that follows.

- Why are you and your colleagues taking this course or reading this book?

- How will this course or book help you in your career?

- How might it help you in other areas of your life?

- Have you any experience in giving presentations? If so, what?

- Do you think you are a good presenter? In what ways?

- What do you feel you need to learn about or practice regarding presentations?

- What do you have to share with your classmates or colleagues about making presentations?

Write about It!

If you are studying alone, write down the answers to these questions and keep your answers in a notebook. Talk about them with a friend or colleague. As you work your way through the book, occasionally look again at your answers to see if you are accomplishing your goals.

If you are in a class, conduct a survey of your classmates. Divide the class into groups of three to seven people. Choose one or two questions (depending on the size of the group) from the preceding list and ask your question(s) of each group member. This form may help you.

Name of Group Member	*Answer*
1. _____	_____
2. _____	_____
3. _____	_____
4. _____	_____

5. _____   _____

6. _____   _____

7. _____   _____

Reassemble as a class. Report the information from your form to the rest of the class.

Are there any conclusions or similarities you can find among your classmates?

YOU'RE ON YOUR WAY!

You have just made a short, informal presentation. Now you are ready to continue through the book to improve your presentation skills. Good luck, and have fun!

Chapter 2

Evaluating Presentations and Giving Feedback

It may seem strange to be thinking about evaluating a presentation before you've even begun to make one! This chapter, however, will give you an overview of the elements of making presentations by helping you learn what qualities make a presentation good. By the end of this chapter, you'll also be in the habit of evaluating every presentation you see as a means to improving your own skills.

EVALUATING PRESENTATIONS

Your skills in making presentations will improve as you become better able to evaluate presentations—both your own and the presentations of others. Ideally, you want to practice your presentations before a real audience, say, a friend, a classmate, or a colleague. Therefore, you need to learn to give and receive feedback.

Furthermore, culture influences what people consider to be a good presentation. If you are making your presentation in a culture different from your own, you need to research the cultural expectations of the audience. Check with your contact person in the target culture for taboo behaviors. Make sure the content of your presentation is appropriate. As a beginning, see appendix A, "Some Information on Specific Cultures for Presenters" (p. 137).

The purpose of the following exercise is to help you think about what makes a good presentation and to help you recognize that other cultures may have different presentation styles.

Think about It!

You may not realize it, but you've observed a lot of presentations in your life. A politician's speech, a salesperson's pitch, an instructor's lecture, a coworker's demonstration are all examples of presentations. As you do the following exercises, think about the presentations you have seen.

3

In your opinion, what makes a presentation good or effective?

In your opinion, what makes a presentation ineffective or not so good?

Compare the list with someone else's list. What similarities did you find? What differences? Are any of your similarities or differences related to the culture you come from?

Similarities	Differences

Now look at the evaluation form in appendix E (p. 147) and compare your lists with the form. Can you think of things to add to your lists?

Use your evaluation form whenever you attend or watch a presentation. Using the form will help you notice things you might have missed and will keep good presentation skills in your mind as you prepare your own presentations.

GIVING AND RECEIVING FEEDBACK

The purpose of feedback is twofold. As you analyze your colleagues' presentations, you learn what makes a good presentation. As you receive feedback, you hone your own skills, thanks to the observant eyes and ears and the kind hearts of your colleagues.

When giving feedback, remember not to be negative or destructive. Choose your language so that you are making constructive, useful statements. Tell your colleague details about what was good in order to reinforce good techniques.

When receiving feedback, even when you disagree with the feedback, realize that something about what you did or said failed to communicate what you wanted. Try to find out how it was that you did not communicate your intended message.

Understand that communication is a difficult thing. People often have to express themselves more than once, and in different ways, in order to get their message across.

Giving Feedback

The purpose of feedback is to help the speaker.

- Try genuinely to find things that will prove useful.

- The more descriptive and more specific you can be, the better.

- Give examples, so the speaker knows precisely what you are referring to.

- Be gentle when giving feedback; don't pile on too much at once so that you overwhelm the speaker.

- Be positive in your tone and attitude.

- Mention something the speaker did well, as well as things the speaker needs to improve.

Receiving Feedback

The purpose of getting feedback is to help you do a better job than you would without the feedback.

- Do not be defensive. Trust the good intentions of the person giving you feedback and be grateful for his or her help.

- Ask for specific examples.

- Repeat, or summarize, the comment to make sure you understand.

- Take notes to help you remember.

Final note: It is up to the receiver to decide what to do with the feedback—to act on it or to disregard it.

WORD BANK

argument (n.), to argue (v.), argumentative (adj.)
criticism (n.), to criticize (v.), critical (adj.)
critique (n.), to critique (v.)

feedback (n.), to give feedback (vp.)
dispute (n.), to dispute (v.)
to be negative (vp.), negative (adj.)
to be positive (vp.), positive (adj.)

Key: n. = noun, v. = verb, vp. = verb phrase, adv. = adverb, adj. = adjective, adj. cmpd. = adjectival compound, syn. = synonym, ant. = antonym

Guess the meanings of the following italicized words from their contexts. Then do the vocabulary exercise following the sentences to check yourself.

1. a. The *argument* Jeremy made to raise his grade was so weak that his teacher lowered it instead.
   b. Noriko *argued* for better food in the cafeteria on the grounds that better food will provide better nutrition.
   c. Fernando's *argumentative* attitude caused his boss to fire him.

What Your Dictionary Might Not Tell You!

A note on usage
To "make an argument" is to give reasons for a position. To "have an argument" or to "get into an argument" is to engage in a verbal fight with someone.

A note on semantics
The noun *argument* and the verb *to argue* can have negative or positive connotations (meanings). The adjective *argumentative* always has a negative connotation.

A note on prepositions
To have an argument *with* someone
To argue *for* or *against* a particular side or position

---

2. a. The journalist's severe *criticism* of the president included his political weakness and his dishonesty.
    b. It hurt his pride when his supervisor *criticized* his writing skills in front of the work team.
    c. The proverb, "Don't break eggs unless you plan to make omelets," advises one not to be unnecessarily *critical*.

What Your Dictionary Might Not Tell You!

A note on prepositions
One makes a critique *of,* or is critical *of,* someone or something.

---

3. The *Times's* *critique* of the play was positive; the theater critic recommended it. But the *Daily News* evaluated the play negatively and panned it.

What Your Dictionary Might Not Tell You!

A note on semantics

- *Critique* is a neutral term that involves a close evaluation of something, looking at both the positive and the negative.
- A *critic,* such as an art *critic* or a food *critic,* makes *critiques* as his or her profession.
- *Criticism* and *critical* generally carry a negative connotation.
- *Critically,* however, does not necessarily carry a negative connotation.

---

4. a. Sam's coworker said so many negative things about Sam's speech that Sam didn't want to hear any *feedback* ever again.
   b. Maria's report improved after her writing partners gave her such useful *feedback*.

5. a. Their *dispute* over the property lines was resolved by the surveyor's report.
   b. Antonio *disputed* the claim that he had cheated, demonstrating that he had followed the rules.

6. a. An enthusiastic approach is better than being *negative* because, as the saying goes, "You can catch more flies with honey than with vinegar."
   b. His disapproving, *negative* outlook discouraged his coworkers.

7. a. Although the bank was having financial problems, the president tried to remain *positive,* assuring the employees that the bank would not close.
   b. His boss's *positive* evaluation of his work on the big project encouraged him to ask for a raise.

Vocabulary Exercise 1—Matching Synonyms

Now that you have made an educated guess about the meanings of the words, match the words on the left with their synonyms on the right. Make certain that you are using the correct forms. Do not use your dictionary!

1. __ feedback (n.)   a. bad; opposite of positive
2. __ argue (v.)   b. to support a particular position or to disagree verbally
3. __ positive (adj.)   c. a response to someone's performance
4. __ critique (v.)   d. good; opposite of negative
5. __ negative (adj.)   e. to express the negative aspects of something
6. __ criticize (v.)   f. to evaluate neutrally, mentioning both the positive and the negative

Now, check your answers with the Answer Key on page 149.

Vocabulary Exercise 2—Using Words in Context

Fill in the blanks with the vocabulary words listed.

negative	argument	critique
feedback	positive	criticism

1. Sae-Won's _____ remarks about my speech made me feel terrible; I wish he had given me more positive comments.

2. After receiving a low grade on the TOEFL test, Anita had a hard time feeling _____ about her chances to study in the United States.

3. Their _____ over who would drive lasted for twenty minutes. Finally, one of their friends ended the dispute by insisting on driving.

4. Getting _____ on a presentation can be very beneficial. It really helps to have another person's opinion about what you can improve on and what you did well.

5. Our instructor asked us to _____ a professional presentation. It was hard to look critically at a professional, but I learned a lot from this experience.

6. Pavel is worried about his annual job review because he has received so much _____ from his boss this year.

Check your answers on page 149.

CROSS-CULTURAL ISSUES

Many cultures consider a criticism of what a person says to be a criticism of that person and maybe even of that person's country or culture. In most northern European heritage cultures (the United Kingdom, Germany, the Netherlands, the Scandinavian countries, the United States, Australia, and New Zealand), however, people tend to separate a criticism of what someone says from the person who says it. People from those cultures believe that an open criticism of an idea, a proposal, or a plan will lead to improving the idea, proposal, or plan. It is even acceptable to criticize the ideas and statements of persons in authority, as long as it is understood to be done with respect and with a goal of improving things.

Some languages are more direct than other languages when making criticisms, complaints, and so on. German and Slavic languages, for instance, tend to be very direct; at the other end of the continuum, Japanese tends to be very indirect; and American English would be somewhere in between. A language speaker from a culture that tends to be very direct when making criticisms or complaints may sound rude to a language speaker from a culture that tends to be less direct— especially if the speaker merely translates from his or her own language, without learning the pragmatics of the second language.

Using modifiers such as "maybe" or "perhaps" in an attempt to soften a criticism is likely to confuse native English speakers, who will, most probably, interpret those words as meaning something less definite than what was intended. An example of this would be the Japanese businessperson giving feedback to an American employee by saying, "Maybe you should change this," when what is really meant is, "You have to change this!" The American will think the boss is making a suggestion that the employee may choose to follow or not.

Now It's Your Turn!

Under what circumstances may someone criticize another person in your culture? If you wanted to give constructive criticism to a colleague, how would you do it?

SAMPLES OF GOOD AND BAD FEEDBACK AND RESPONSES TO FEEDBACK

Giving Feedback

Read the following examples of feedback and think about what makes them useful or useless. Refer to the list titled "Giving Feedback" on page 5, earlier in this chapter.

1. "Maria, you started out speaking loudly and clearly, but, the farther you went, you began speaking more and more softly, so that, by the end of your presentation, I had trouble hearing you."

    ___ useful ___ useless

    Why? _____

    _____

    _____

2. "Your arguments are stupid! No one would believe them."

___ useful ___ useless

Why? _____

_____

_____

3. "José, I found your organization, in general, to be very good. However, in the second section of your presentation, when you were talking about the reasons for delaying the project, you started talking about the prices, and I couldn't understand why you included that information in that section."

___ useful ___ useless

Why? _____

_____

_____

4. "I thought everything in the presentation was just fine."

___ useful ___ useless

Why? _____

_____

_____

Responding to Feedback

Read the following examples of responses and think about what makes them good or bad. Refer to the list titled "Receiving Feedback" on page 5, earlier in this chapter.

1. "Oh! I hadn't even noticed that I wasn't looking at the audience. I guess I got a little nervous. I think I will have to make a note on my notes to remember to make appropriate eye contact."

___ good ___ bad

Why? _____

_____

_____

2. "I think my organization is perfectly clear; it doesn't need changing."

__ good __ bad

Why? _____

_____

_____

3. "Hm. I see. Perhaps I need to explain why discussing prices is necessary in that section—or maybe I should move it to a different section. I'll have to think about that. Thanks for drawing my attention to it."

__ good __ bad

Why? _____

_____

_____

4. Silence.

__ good __ bad

Why? _____

_____

_____

PRESENTATION EXERCISE

Look at the following topics, then choose one and prepare a presentation.

- The best job you ever had and what made it good
- The worst job you ever had and what made it bad
- The first job you ever had and what you learned from it
- The industry you work in or would like to work in
- A topic of your choice

Note: When choosing a topic, remember that, the more you know about what you talk about and the more interested you are in it, the easier it will be to give the presentation—and the better it will be!

Use the Presentation Planning Guide at the end of the chapter (p. 14) to help you plan your speech.

If possible, have someone videotape your presentation.

OBSERVE AND GIVE FEEDBACK

Step 1. If you are in a class, watch your classmates' presentations. If you are not part of a class, watch your own videotaped presentation or find a local presentation to watch. (For information on how to find local presentations, see appendix B, "Additional Resources," page 141.) Based on your lists from earlier in the chapter of what makes a good presentation, think about the presentation and write a critique of the presentation in the following chart. List the strengths and weaknesses and make suggestions for improvement.

Strengths	Weaknesses	Suggestions

Step 2. Give feedback to the presenter. Refer to the list titled "Giving Feedback" on page 5. If you are working alone, think about your presentation. Give yourself feedback. It is usually harder to be objective with yourself, so remember to follow the instructions about giving feedback. Do not overwhelm yourself with what you think is bad about the presentation. Look first for what was good.

Step 3. When the class or a friend gives feedback to you, how should you respond? Practice receiving feedback graciously. Refer to the list titled "Receiving Feedback" on page 5.

Presentation Planning Guide

Before you begin, think about these questions.
- What is the purpose or intended outcome of the presentation?
- Who is your audience?

Introduction
- What grabber (something to catch the interest of your audience) will you start with?
- What are your topic and focus? By the end of your introduction, your audience should know what your topic is and have a basic expectation of what you will be talking about. Your focus should be clear.
- What background information will your audience need to know to understand this presentation?

Body
- Support your topic with examples, statistics, or anecdotes (stories).
- What terms might your audience need defined?
- Use visual aids whenever possible.

Conclusion
- Leave your audience with something to remember. Repeat your main idea.

Something to keep in mind
- Never lose sight of your main idea. The audience needs to have a clear idea of the purpose of your speech. Let your introduction lead them there, and let your conclusion reinforce it.

Chapter 3

Planning the Presentation

The better the planning, the better the presentation! Prepare to spend time thinking about what you are going to do during your presentation.

Purpose. The first step is to decide what the purpose, or objective, of your presentation is. Why are you making this presentation? What do you hope to accomplish with it? What are the expected results? Are you training new employees to use a piece of equipment? Are you trying to convince your boss to expand your product line? Are you encouraging your team members to sell more than they sold last year?

Type. Once you know the purpose of your presentation, you will know what type of presentation it will be. It may be an informative presentation, a persuasive one, or an inspirational one. (Most presentations will fit into one of these general categories.) The information, organization, and language will all be affected by the type of presentation you are making.

Genre. Next, you must choose the most appropriate genre of presentation. Are you describing something, telling a chronological narrative, or explaining a process? Do you have a main point or topic you need to cover?

Length. Consider the length of your presentation. First, what is the amount of time it will take to do a good job of making your presentation? Second, will any time limits be imposed on you? That is, will you be given a certain length of time? Will there, for instance, be a certain amount of time allotted to this meeting?

Audience. The most important thing to consider, once you have the purpose of your presentation in mind, is your audience. Before you begin preparing your presentation, you have to have a clear idea of who your audience will be. Why are they there—what do they expect to get out of your presentation? What background information do they have on your topic? Do they speak your native language?

Logistics. How large will your audience be? Will it be a small group sitting around a table or a large group in a big auditorium? What is the room like? Was it built for making presentations, or is it a small, narrow storeroom? What are its acoustics like? Is there a podium, a microphone, or built-in visual aid equipment and facilities? Both your content and your presentation style will be affected by the size of your audience and what the room is like.

Careful consideration of your audience is necessary for an effective presentation. Even the best presentation will fail if the audience has not been considered.

Think about It!

You are giving a presentation introducing your company. How would you modify your talk to accommodate the following audiences?

1. Your eight-year-old niece's school class
2. A group of new employees
3. A prospective client
4. College students attending Career Day
5. Your family members

By looking at these examples, you can see that the audience profoundly influences your presentation. For example, with the eight-year-old children, you would probably use lots of visual aids, ask many questions, and perhaps initiate some role play on the part of the children. If you were giving a presentation to new employees, you would discuss different information, in greater detail, with more sophisticated and more technical language than you would with the children—and your visual aids would contain different information. A presentation to a prospective client would be more formal than the presentation given to your family. Thus, your language, your style, and the content of your presentation change from audience to audience.

For Career Day, you are trying to encourage the listeners to consider working for your company; with the new employees, you are trying to build a sense of ingroup identity and team spirit; for your family, you want them to feel proud of what you are doing. The purpose of your presentation will vary with different audiences.

WORD BANK

to allot (v.), allotted (adj.)	stationery (n.)
profound (adj.), profoundly (adv.)	to fall through (idiom)
appropriate (adj.), appropriately (adv.)	acoustics (n.)

Guess the meanings of the following italicized words from their contexts. Then do the vocabulary exercises following the sentences to check yourself.

1. a. Jerry sold all the tickets he had been *allotted,* so he borrowed some of Ahmed's share.
   b. The time *allotted* was up, so the committee had to continue another day.

2. a. Being fired from his first job had a *profound* effect on Michel—he never got over it.
   b. The generosity of the company affected the employees *profoundly* and produced strong loyalty in them.

3. a. That salary is an *appropriate* remuneration for that position—if the workload changes, we'll consider changing the salary.
   b. Juanita always behaved *appropriately;* you could trust her to do the right thing.

4. Now that we have a joint venture with BigBucks Sporting Goods, we have to design new *stationery* so the letters will go out under both company names.

What Your Dictionary Might Not Tell You!

Stationery and *stationary* are pronounced the same in most major English dialects.

Stationery refers to the paper used specifically for correspondence (for letters and memos), and *stationary* means "not moving."

---

5. The travel plans for the holidays *fell through* and we ended up staying home.

6. The *acoustics* of the room were so good that I didn't need a microphone.

Vocabulary Exercise 1—Definitions

In the answer blanks, write what you think the words mean.

1. allot _____

2. profound _____

3. appropriate _____

4. to fall through _____

5. acoustics _____

Check your answers on page 149.

Vocabulary Exercise 2—Matching Antonyms

Now that you have made an educated guess about the meanings of the words, match the words on the left with their antonyms on the right. Make certain that you are using the correct forms. Do not use your dictionary!

1. ___ to fall through (v.)   a.   succeed
2. ___ appropriate (adj.)   b.   shallow
3. ___ profound (adj.)   c.   not given
4. ___ allotted (adj.)   d.   objectionable

Check your answers on page 149.

GRAMMAR REVIEW—MODALS

Modals can be among the trickiest of forms to learn because the usage is so varied. There is often overlap, and different aspects of the modals are on a sliding scale. However, incorrect use of modals can cause serious misunderstandings, and so learners need to pay close attention whenever they hear modals used.

have to indicates

- spatial or temporal limits or other natural limits ("I have to do it today, because tomorrow is the deadline, and then it will be too late." "We have to take a different route, because the storm has washed out the road.")

- laws, rules, and regulations ("I have to obey the speed limit on this road, or I could get a very expensive ticket." "We have to pay our electricity bill, or they'll cut off the electricity." "The only things you have to do are die and pay taxes!")

- an obligation with some kind of penalty if you don't do it ("If you want to have a good business relationship with O'Leary, here's what you have to do . . ." "I have to wash my hair tonight—or else I'll look terrible tomorrow.")

- strong deduction or conclusion in opposition to contrary evidence ("I can't find my notes for the meeting, but they *have* to be here somewhere!" "I don't care what you say, she *has* to have left the building! We've looked everywhere, and she's just not here!" "There *has* to be another explanation—this just doesn't make any sense!")

Note: *Have to* is <u>extremely</u> common in spoken English. Do not confuse *have to* with *should*. While there are times of overlap ("I *should* wash my hair tonight— or else I'll look terrible tomorrow"), the more serious the penalty, the more you should use *have to*. Always use *have to* with laws and regulations. Also, do not confuse this modal with the verb *to have*.

must indicates

- necessity ("Hard hats must be worn in this area") or

- a deduction ("That must be the cab now." "She must have missed the plane.")

  Note: In American English, *must* in the sense of necessity is rarely used in spoken situations. It is used in formal or literary writing, regulations, signs, and other documents.

should indicates

- a good idea, a recommendation, a suggestion ("You should try this restaurant for business lunches. They have private rooms available and give great service") or

- a prediction or deduction (including a scientific experiment or a process such as cooking) ("Jones is always on time, so he should be arriving any minute now." "Your luggage should be safe there overnight." "This subject shouldn't be too controversial for this crowd.")

- a moral or social obligation without serious consequences ("I should iron my shirt tonight, because I'll be too tired in the morning"; "I should study harder in my classes, but a B average is all I need.") or

be + supposed to indicates

- an expectation ("We're supposed to eat dinner with Great-Aunt Marie on Tuesday, but we can postpone that to another time.")

- a moral or social obligation without serious consequences ("I'm supposed to attend religious services every week, but I usually don't go that regularly.")

  Note: Do not confuse *be + supposed to* with the verb *to suppose*.
  <u>General guideline:</u> If the expectation or obligation comes from outside oneself, or from a rule imposed on the speaker, *be + supposed to* will <u>usually</u> be used, instead of *should*. *Should* is <u>generally</u> used when the expectation or obligation has been internalized.

need to indicates

- a need or obligation, sometimes urgent ("We need to get her to the hospital immediately!") or serious ("I need to do payroll today"); sometimes less urgent ("You need to start planning for that trip next month") or less serious ("I need to get a haircut.")

Comparative examples

- I *am supposed to* go to the concert; my friend is performing in it. *Meaning:* My friend expects me to go and hear him.

- I *should* go to the concert; my friend is performing in it. *Meaning:* My friend may be disappointed if I don't go, but it won't ruin our friendship.

- I *need to/have to/must* go to the concert; my friend is performing in it. *Meaning:* My friend will be so upset if I don't go that it will ruin our friendship.

Grammar Exercise—Modals

Fill in the blanks with *should, be + supposed to, have to,* or *must.* Use the context to determine the answer. Be ready to explain why you chose your answer.

1. I _____ write monthly reports for all the other departments. But, if I don't do it, nothing happens.

2. I _____ write these monthly reports for all the other departments, because, if I don't get them this information, we could lose a lot of money.

3. She _____ have already left for lunch, because her office is empty and her coat is gone.

4. This paper in the garbage _____ have gone through the shredder—it's in tiny pieces.

5. My doctor told me I _____ start working out regularly, or I could have a heart attack from the stress on my job.

6. I _____ call my customer as soon as I can find a phone, or else I will lose that sale!

7. I _____ call my customer and congratulate him on his daughter's graduation—just as a polite gesture.

8. Thor _____ pick up the group at the airport because he knows the best route around the construction.

9. Thor _____ pick up the group at the airport—I heard Harry asking him.

10. Thor _____ pick up the group at the airport—no one else can drive!

11. The plane _____ have been here an hour ago, according to the schedule.

12. We _____ order more memo stationery soon because we're getting low.

Now, check your answers on page 149.

As you prepare your presentation, pay special attention to your use of these modals.

PRESENTATION EXERCISE

Either in class or working alone: Make a short presentation about your job. Choose one of the following audiences and focus your presentation for that audience. Ask your classmates or a friend to guess which audience you are speaking to.

- Your grandmother

- Someone who does your job in another company

- A college class studying your business

- The person who will move into your position after you have been promoted

- A group of ten-year-old children

- A person you want to hire

Remember to think about the purpose of the presentation, that is, what you hope to achieve. Will it be informational, persuasive, or inspirational? How long should it last?

Use this checklist to help you prepare.

Checklist for Successful Planning

___ Begin planning your presentation as soon as possible.
___ Determine the expected outcome(s) of your presentation.
___ Based on the expected outcome(s), decide whether your presentation will be informational, persuasive, or inspirational.
___ Find out how much background the audience has in your topic.
___ If your audience is from a culture different from your own, research their expectations.
___ Learn how much time is allotted for your presentation.
___ Find out the size of your audience.
___ Visit the room you will be using or get a description of it.
___ Plan what kind of visual aids you will use.
___ Have a backup plan for unexpected problems or last-minute changes.

OBSERVE AND GIVE FEEDBACK

Watch a presentation at work or at school or on television. Evaluate the presentation in terms of the speaker's planning, purpose, style, and response to the audience. Use this work sheet to record your opinions.

---

1. Was the purpose of the presentation clear?

2. Was it an informational, a persuasive, or an inspirational presentation?

3. Was it appropriate for the audience?

4. Was the length too short, too long, or just right?

CROSS-CULTURAL ISSUES

Learn to distinguish between hearsay and legitimate cross-cultural information. When research has been done according to strict scholarly rules and the information has been determined to be *statistically valid,* you can probably trust that information to be accurate. The opinion of a person who has made a short visit to a country may be interesting but may also not be reliable, or the limited experience of that person may not be generalizable. Culture is a complex thing—it takes a long time and a lot of study to be able to understand a culture. Sometimes, even a person who lives in a culture may not be able to give *statistically valid* information about his or her culture, although such a person generally is more reliable than someone from outside the culture.

One way to tell the difference is that hearsay is usually superficial in its evidence and explanation—and can lead to stereotyping. Statistically valid information is backed up by scholarly research done by people who have been trained in the field and who know how to interpret their results. Valid cultural information leads to an understanding of the culture and its values.

For additional discussion of valid cultural information in a business context, see appendix C, "Bibliography on Business and Culture" (p. 143).

Chapter 4

Research

WORD BANK

periodical (n.), periodic (adj.), periodically (adv.)
primary source/data (np.)
secondary source/data (np.)
market research (np.)
subjective (adj.), subjectively (adv.)
objective (adj.), objectively (adv.)

the Internet (n.)
World Wide Web (np.)
electronic mail (e-mail) (np.)
archives (n.), to archive (v.)
curator (n.)

Guess the meanings of the following italicized words from their contexts. Then do the vocabulary exercise following the sentences to check yourself.

1. a. All three of these magazines are published *periodically*—this one comes out weekly; this one, monthly; and this last one, every other month.
    b. We have to send in *periodic* reports to the main office; the timing depends on which report you're talking about.
    c. The *periodical* section of the library holds magazines and journals.

2. The *curator* repairs old manuscripts and generally takes care of the collection.

3. a. All that information is stored in the *archives.*
    b. You can *archive* that report on-line with all the previous reports.

4. The folks in the marketing department are always doing *market research,* collecting and analyzing information about their target market.

5. They did original research, going to *primary sources* for their information, not just to other collections of information.

6. Using *secondary sources,* like information from the Census Bureau, is acceptable for this report.

7. a. It was his *subjective* opinion that all Americans are superficial; but I don't think the facts back him up.
    b. Teachers try not to grade *subjectively.* They base the grades on the students' work and don't let their feelings affect the grades.

8. a. The boss says he wants an *objective* report on our hiring practices—he wants the facts and arguments on both sides of the issue.

   b. He was speaking *objectively* when he said, "The evidence is overwhelmingly in my opponent's favor."

Vocabulary Exercise—Using the Words in Context

Write a paragraph about doing research in which you use all the vocabulary words in one coherent whole.

Exercise—Subjective versus Objective

A *subjective* opinion is based on one's emotions or personal experience.
An *objective* opinion is based on an emotionally detached observation or on demonstrable facts.

   Read the following sentences. Write an S next to the sentences that you think are subjective and an O next to the ones that you think are objective.

___ 1. Studies at the University of Minnesota have shown that, if you stand up and give a presentation with visual aids, your audience is 43% more likely to be persuaded.

___ 2. I think you should be paid a higher salary.

___ 3. Based on the industry average, as reported in the most recent professional newsletter, you should be getting a higher salary.

___ 4. Everyone knows that children learn languages faster than adults.

___ 5. Industry observers are predicting a hard year ahead for Apple Computers.

Check your answers on page 150.

Language Tip

You can start a sentence that states your opinion with, "Speaking subjectively. . . ."

PRESENTATION EXERCISE

Prepare to give a presentation about doing research. If you are working on your own, fill out all of the forms (pp. 27–30). If you are working with a class, work on the forms in groups and, later, make a group presentation.

The best way to improve your research skills and learn about research tools is actually to experience using them. The following exercise will help you discover several of the research areas available to you.

Exercise: Learning about Research Tools

(Where can I get the information I need?)

If you are in a class, do exercise A. If you are working alone, do exercise B.

A. Working with a Class

Step 1.   You will be divided into groups. Each group will make a presentation to the rest of the class about some research tools. The purpose of the presentation is to inform your classmates of the various research items available.

Step 2.   Each group should choose one of the research task forms. Then divide up the questions in your form so that each member of your group is responsible for finding out a specific part of the information.

Step 3.   Gather your information.

Step 4.   After each individual has gathered the information, meet and decide how you will organize your presentation for the class. Use the Presentation Planning Guide (p. 33) to help you organize your speeches. Concentrate on clarity and brevity. Remember, your audience's time is limited. They want to find out the greatest amount of information in the shortest amount of time.

Step 5.   Practice your presentation. Look over the Peer/Self-Evaluation sheet at the end of the chapter (p. 34) to evaluate your group's performance.

Step 6.   After you give your group presentation, carefully look over the peer responses to determine what areas you can improve in your next presentation.

B. Working on Your Own

Step 1.   Decide which areas of research in the list of research tasks you know the least about. Choose one of them and prepare a presentation on it.

Step 2. After you have gathered the information, decide how you will organize your presentation. Use the Presentation Planning Guide (p. 33) to help you organize your speech. Concentrate on clarity and brevity. You want to give the greatest amount of information in the shortest amount of time.

Step 3. Practice your presentation. Look over the Peer/Self-Evaluation sheet at the end of the chapter (p. 34) to help you prepare.

Step 4. Tape-record or videotape your presentation.

Research Tasks

Choose among the following research tasks: library research, electronic research, museum research, local company research, or local organization research. Use the forms (pages 27–30) to help you collect and organize your information.

Library Research Form

Visit your local public, university, or company library. Investigate the answers to these questions.

1. What computer research equipment does the library have? Databases? CD-ROMs? Explain the use of each system.

2. What newspapers relevant to your class or individual needs does the library subscribe to?

3. What periodicals or newsletters relevant to your class or individual needs does the library subscribe to?

Electronic Research Form

1. What electronic facilities do you have access to in your community, university, and/or business?

2. What forms of Internet access are available (i.e., World Wide Web, FTP (File Transfer Protocol), e-mail, newsgroups, etc.)?

3. Write a brief bibliography to be distributed to your classmates of the most current Internet resources.

4. What human resources are available to assist with research over the Internet (i.e., 800 numbers, local university support, usergroups)?

Museum Research Form

Make an appointment to visit with the curator of a museum. The curator can help you answer the following questions.

1. Does the museum have any open archives available to the public?

2. If so, where are the archives located, and what is the procedure for examining them?

3. Does the museum have an educational program?

4. Does the museum have additional resources available to a researcher?

Local Company Research Form

Pick a company of mutual interest to your group.

1. Does the company give tours?

2. Does the company have resources available to outside researchers?

3. Does the company provide educational speakers?

Local Organizations Research Form

Pick a community organization of mutual interest to your group. **Suggestions:** Professional groups, International Rotary Club, Girl Scouts, Boy Scouts, Small Business Administration, Chambers of Commerce, charities (such as your local Red Cross or Red Crescent group).

1. Does the organization have resources available to the public?

2. Does the organization publish books or brochures of use to you or the class?

Interviewing can be one of the best research tools.

Tips for Interviewing People

A research tool often overlooked is interviewing professionals and experts who know about the topic you are researching. This can be one of the best ways to get solid, useful, and up-to-date information. Here are a few tips for a successful interview.

1. Do research to make sure you find the right person to talk to.
2. Find out what the person's background is concerning the topic; learn something about the person's company if the company is in a related business.
3. Call the person to ask for an interview.
4. Assure him or her that you will only take 20 minutes of his or her time.
5. Prepare your questions ahead of time, based on your background research.
6. Thank the interviewee for having taken the time to help you, and send a written thank you note the next day.

OBSERVE AND GIVE FEEDBACK

If you videotaped your presentation, evaluate it. Was it well planned? Was the research adequate? What areas can you improve upon for your next presentation? Use the Peer/Self-Evaluation form at the end of the chapter (p. 34).

CROSS-CULTURAL ISSUES

Freedom of information and access to information vary from culture to culture and country to country. The assumption that information should be publicly available does not exist everywhere. Information on businesses may be less readily available in some countries than in others because it hasn't been collected. (This is often true in NIS (newly independent states) countries, for example.) Varying accounting practices also influence which information is available. (Germany, the United States, and the United Kingdom all use different accounting systems, for instance.)

In some cultures, for example, in Taiwan, it is essential to have a contact in a company before you can get any information about the company—and, even then, you may not be given much information. In some countries, for example, India, Indonesia, and Romania, people are unaccustomed to filling out surveys and questionnaires or to answering questions by census takers.

With the advent of the World Wide Web, the ability to access information has been acutely democratized. More and more information is becoming available to more and more people with fewer and fewer controls. Technology cuts across cultural assumptions.

Now It's Your Turn

1. What information is and is not readily available in your country or the country in which you are studying?

2. Why is certain information hard to find in your country or the country in which you are studying?

Presentation Planning Guide

Before you begin, think about these questions.
- What is the purpose or intended outcome of the presentation?
- Who is your audience?
- What is the expected length?

Introduction
- Begin with something that captures the interest of your audience. Give them a reason to listen to you.
  Example: "Did you realize that just four blocks away at the public library there is an invaluable source of information on your favorite topic?" or "Just last year, I had never used a computer, but now I've learned to let my computer link me to the world."
- By the end of your introduction, your audience should know what your topic is and have a basic expectation of what you will be talking about.

Body
- Give your information and supporting details.
- Explain clearly the use and importance of the research facilities and tools, as well as how to access them.
- Give the location of the facility or tool.
- Define terms that your audience might not be familiar with.
- Use visual aids, such as a printout of a screen from the search on the computer, whenever possible.

Conclusion
- Leave your audience with a solid understanding of your main points and something to remember.
  Example: "The number of usergroups in your field is increasing daily. Here's how to find them . . ."

Things to keep in mind
- Visual aids help your audience understand and remember your presentation better. A map of the library or a brief diagram explaining the Internet can help your audience visualize your explanations.
- Use every member of your group in some way during the presentation.

Peer/Self-Evaluation Form

1. Was the presentation informative?
   __ yes __ no __ somewhat
   Comments:

2. If visual aids were used, were they clear and easy to understand?
   __ yes __ no __ somewhat
   Comments:

3. Do you know where to locate the research tool that was being presented?
   __ yes __ no
   Comments:

4. Was the presentation well planned? Did the presenter use language appropriate for the audience?

5. What one thing do you remember from the presentation?

Chapter 5

Brainstorming and Focusing

WORD BANK

topic (n.)	the subject, theme
thesis (n.)	proposition or conclusion to be supported or argued
broad topic (np.)	a general, extensive, large theme or subject
narrow topic (np.)	a specific, confined, limited theme or subject
to focus (v.)	to specify, clarify, target, to hone in on
objective (n.)	the goal, aim, target
to dissuade (v.)	to convince against, to deter, to talk out of
analysis (n.)	a critique or close study of something
definitive (adj.)	complete and authoritative, conclusive
brainstorming (n.)	the process of coming up with as many ideas—both good and bad—as possible without stopping to judge them (evaluation comes later in the process)

A good presentation is balanced. That is, it contains the right amount of the right kinds of information. It can be easy to choose a topic that is too broad to cover in the time allotted or, if given a topic, to try to talk about it in too much detail. This chapter gives you ideas and exercises to help you develop a balanced presentation.

Tip

Knowing the purpose of the presentation will help you narrow your topic. Knowing the time limitations will help you both narrow your topic and gauge the depth of detail to cover in your topic. Sometimes, your time limits will prevent you from covering the topic in as much detail as you or your audience would like. (In that case, acknowledge the aspects that you will not be able to cover due to time constraints.)

Model:
Topic ⇒ Brainstorming ⇒ Focusing

The first step is to choose a general topic. The next step is to brainstorm about that topic, producing a lot of ideas based on the information you gained in your research. Then you focus.

CHOOSING A TOPIC

Choose from the following topics.

- The industry you work in or would like to work in

- The GATT (General Agreement on Tariffs and Trade) or ASEAN (the Association of Southeast Asian Nations) or another international business organization

- International currency issues in international business

- Establishing a new business

- Your country

- A topic of your choice

TECHNIQUES FOR BRAINSTORMING AND FOCUSING

Brainstorming is a process for coming up with ideas that you might not think of otherwise and that you can use in your presentations and writing. It is a way to flesh out your presentation and make it richer. Brainstorming can help you develop a topic and come up with supporting information for the body of the presentation and innovative ways to begin and end your presentation.

There are many brainstorming techniques; here are three. See which ones work best for you.

Brainstorming Technique 1—Freewriting

Write your topic here _____.

Then, in the space provided on page 37, write for ten minutes about your topic. Write whatever you think of about your topic in whatever random order the ideas pop up. Do not worry about grammar, spelling, punctuation, or anything except your topic.

Brainstorming Technique 2—Spontaneous Generation

Spontaneous thinking is most effective when done with two or more people but can also be done alone. It consists of coming up with as many ideas (related or not) as possible and writing them down in no particular order. Doing this on a blackboard or a very large sheet of paper helps you keep your creativity flowing. Do not stop to discuss or organize or evaluate your ideas while brainstorming. Every idea that anyone suggests gets written down. There are no wrong or bad ideas while doing spontaneous thinking. Write until no one can think of any more ideas.

Brainstorming Technique 3—Mind Mapping (Webbing)

Mind Mapping, or Webbing, is used here to describe a technique to help you organize the flow of information in your mind that relates to your topic.

Here is an example of a Mind Map that could be drawn by a tour director planning a speech for tourists visiting a famous lighthouse.

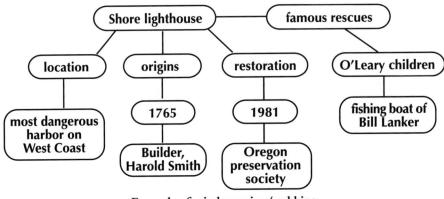

Example of mindmapping/webbing

There is no right or wrong way to organize a Mind Map. Just try to follow the flow of your thoughts.

With your chosen topic in mind, do some brainstorming with one of these methods.

Look through the results of your brainstorming. There should be a lot of ideas and information. Now, you need to focus those ideas and the information to fit the purpose and time limits of your presentation. Look back at what you've written and decide what part of your topic you would like to talk about, with your purpose and time limits in mind.

After you finish brainstorming, you are ready to focus all those ideas and come up with the main idea for your presentation. Some individuals do not have trouble deciding what they want to talk about. For those who do, the following techniques are designed to help focus or narrow a topic. Try all of the techniques, using different topics, and then decide which ones work best for you.

Technique 1 for Narrowing Topic—Diagram and Question

First, you diagram your topic, and then you ask yourself a series of questions to narrow your topic further. Here is a model of the diagram.

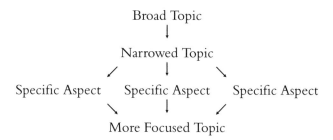

Questions

a. What general topic do I want or need to talk about?
b. Who is my audience?
c. What do they expect to hear?
d. What do they need to hear? (That is, what do I want them to understand from my speech? Is it the same thing as what they expect to hear?)
e. How much time do I have for my presentation?

After diagramming your topic and answering the questions, you should begin to have a good idea of what your focused topic, your main idea, will be.

Follow the specific example below.

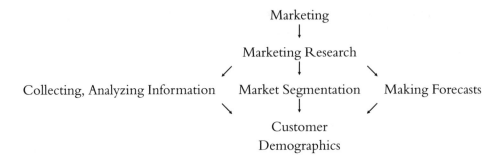

Questions

a. What general topic do I want or need to talk about? *Marketing*
b. Who is my audience? *Analysts from the finance department*
c. What do they expect to hear? *A general update from the marketing department*
d. What do they need to hear? *The reason our customers can't pay the high price for a certain product that we are currently marketing*
e. What is the time limit? *20 minutes*
f. What is my focused topic? *Customer demographics*

Here's another one (this time the audience's needs and expectations are the same).

Audience: Head of auditing department

Expects to hear: A recommendation for solving problems in the auditing department

Needs to hear: A recommendation for solving problems in the auditing department

Time limit: 30 minutes

General topic (too broad): Computers

Still too broad: Computers in the workplace

Better: How computers improve productivity in the workplace

Best: Improving performance in the auditing department by switching to personal computers (PCs)

Focusing Exercise

Fill in as many blanks as you wish.

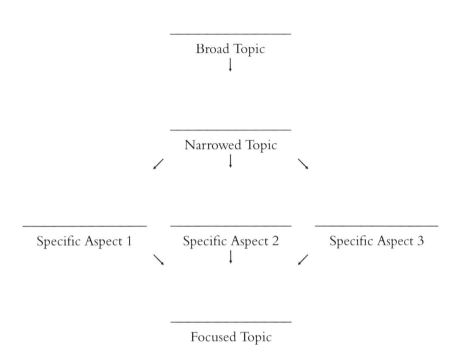

Questions
a. Who is my audience?
b. What do they expect to hear?
c. What do they need or want to hear?
d. Time limits?
e. Focused topic?

Technique 2 for Narrowing Topic—Goals and Objectives

Different techniques work better for different people; so, here's another technique
to try.

Model:
Goal → Objective → Strategic Question → Analysis of Audience → Focus

Begin with what you want to accomplish, that is, your goal. What do you want the result or outcome of your presentation to be?

Example Goal: To enlarge the number of people who distribute my product.

Next, ask yourself: what step(s) do I (we) need to take to reach the goal? These intermediate, doable steps are your objectives.

Example Objective: To convince at least 25 people out of an audience of 100 to distribute Fountain of Youth health care product.

Next, you need to determine your strategy, or, how to meet your objective. To do this, turn your objective into a question.

Example Objective-Turned-into-a-Question: What will convince the audience to distribute my products?

Strategizing leads to an analysis of your audience (see chap. 3, "Planning the Presentation"). What do you know about your audience? This may involve talking with the sponsors of your presentation or doing an informal survey. If people are paying to hear your presentation, it is best to send out a survey before the event.

Example Analysis: Group of slightly experienced salespeople, ready to find a new product to sell

The analysis of your audience and your objective helps you decide what you will focus on in your speech.

Example Focus: The speech will emphasize distributor support and training that makes the product easy to sell.

Now, using your topic from the beginning of the chapter, set your own goal and identify your objectives.

Your goal

Your objectives

Now, turn your objective into a strategic question.

Analyze your audience

Your focus

Vocabulary Review Exercise—Crossword Puzzle

Across

1. a specific, confined, limited topic (two words)
3. a proposition to be defended
5. the process of coming up with as many ideas as possible without stopping to judge them
6. a critique or close study of something
8. complete and authoritative; conclusive
9. a general, extensive, large topic (two words)

Down

2. the goal, aim, target
4. to convince against, to deter, to talk out of
7. the subject, theme
10. to specify, clarify, hone in on (two words)

Check your answers on page 150.

CROSS-CULTURAL ISSUES

In making presentations, when and how you get to your goal varies from culture to culture. In some cultures, such as Malaysia, you have to spend time in your presentation acknowledging the important people in your audience before getting down to talking about the focus of your presentation.

In Germany and the United States, it is important to be very specific and clear—up front—about the focus of your topic, but in Taiwan and Japan, it is common to talk around—offer impressions about—the general theme of the topic and let the audience figure out what is being said.

In some cultures, such as those in Japan, Taiwan, and Mexico, it is important to establish a personal working relationship before getting down to business. You may meet many times with people who may become your clients or business partners before being allowed to make a presentation that focuses on your main goal. In northern European cultures, however, you can get down to business right away—sometimes meeting a person for the first time, making a deal, and leaving the same day.

Now It's Your Turn

Think about presentations that you have heard in your own country. How are they organized? When is the main idea introduced? How does the speaker handle the audience?

PRESENTATION EXERCISE

Using the focused topic that you have worked with here, make a speech. Use the Presentation Planning Guide to plan your speech and use the Peer/Self-Evaluation form for feedback.

Presentation Planning Guide

Before I begin, I will think about these questions.
- What is the purpose, goal, or intended outcome of the presentation?
- What steps must I take (objectives) to reach my goal?
- Who is my audience? (what strategy must I follow?)
- What is the expected length of my presentation?

Introduction
- What grabber will I start with to catch my audience's attention?
- What are my topic and focus? (By the end of your introduction, your audience should know what your topic is and have a basic expectation of what you will be talking about. Your focus should be clear.)
- What background information will my audience need to know in order to understand the presentation?

Body
- How will I support my arguments? Examples? Statistics? Anecdotes (stories)?
- What terms might my audience need defined?
- What visual aids can I use?

Conclusion
- What one, main idea do I want to leave my audience thinking about?

Something to keep in mind
- I will never lose sight of my topic. The audience will have a clear idea of the purpose of my speech; the introduction will lead them to my purpose, and the conclusion will reinforce it.

Peer/Self-Evaluation Form

1. What did the speaker use to grab the audience's attention?

2. What was the topic of the presentation?

3. Was there enough time for the topic to be covered? (Was it too broad?)

4. Was there too little information to fill the time? (Was the topic too narrow?)

5. Did the speaker support the topic with examples, statistics, or stories?
   __ yes __ no __ somewhat

6. Did the speaker define terms and give other background information as needed?

7. What was the speaker's purpose?

   Comments:

Chapter 6

Types of Rhetoric—Persuading, Informing, Inspiring

WORD BANK

rhetoric (n.), rhetorical (adj.), rhetorically (adv.)

rhetorical question (np.)

predominant (adj.), predominantly (adv.)

inspiration (n.), to inspire (v.), inspirational (adj.)

contention (n.), to contend (v.)

pros and cons (n.)

reason, reasoning (n.), to reason (v.), to reason (well or poorly) (vp.), well or poorly reasoned (adj.), to be reasonable (vp.)

logic (n.), to be logical (vp.), logical (adj.), illogical (ant.)

to close a sale/deal (idiom)

Guess the meanings of the following italicized words from their contexts. Then do the vocabulary exercises following the sentences to check yourself.

1. a. *Rhetoric* is a word and concept used by the ancient Greeks to describe the style of speaking used by senators when they were trying to convince their fellows to agree with them.
   b. *Rhetorical* speaking and writing are essential in marketing, where the goal is to persuade people to purchase a product.
   c. She's speaking *rhetorically* now, trying to influence the decision of the committee.

2. A speaker who uses *rhetorical questions* during a presentation helps the audience think about the point being made without having to interrupt the presentation to answer the questions.

3. a. That company has been the *predominant* one in this industry for over ten years—it's time someone challenged their control of the market!
   b. They do business *predominantly* in the north of the country.

4. a. Jack's ability to keep his company alive despite extremely difficult circumstances was an *inspiration* to all of us who hoped to succeed with our own companies.

b. The enthusiastic response of Tony's grandmother *inspired* him to follow his dream and start his own restaurant.

c. *Inspirational* speakers are sometimes hired by companies to improve morale among the employees.

5. a. It was her *contention* that she had been passed over for the job because she was a woman.

b. Despite opposition by the marketing department, I *contend* that our company ought to extend its sales into Asia.

What Your Dictionary Might Not Tell You!

A note on grammar
Contend is a stative verb, that is, it does not take the progressive form.

---

6. Vladimir considered the *pros and cons* of renting and decided that the positives outweighed the negatives.

What Your Dictionary Might Not Tell You!

A note on prepositions
One talks about the pros and cons *of* something.

---

7. a. Tom's *well-reasoned* argument convinced his roommate to go back to school.

b. The *reasoning* in the general's speech did not demonstrate a logical process.

c. The police officer *reasoned* with the gunman until he calmed down and released the hostages.

What Your Dictionary Might Not Tell You!

A note on prepositions
One reasons *with* someone, and *for* or *against* ideas.

8. a. Too much emotion and not enough *logic* in her argument left them unconvinced.

   b. Sherlock Holmes is famous for his *logical* thinking because he was able to deduce the identity of a criminal from tiny fragments of evidence.

9. After weeks of preliminary discussions, the two airlines finally agreed to coshare certain routes. They *closed the deal* yesterday.

Vocabulary Exercise 1—Matching Synonyms

Now that you have made an educated guess about the meanings of the words, match the words on the left with their synonyms on the right. Make certain that you are using the correct forms. Do not use your dictionary!

1. ___ rational (adj.)	a.	the science of correct reasoning
2. ___ logic (n.)	b.	disadvantages and advantages of something; for and against
3. ___ pros and cons (n.)		
4. ___ to reason (v.)	c.	reasonable; using rationality as opposed to emotions
5. ___ to contend (v.)		
6. ___ to close the deal (vp.)	d.	to claim; to assert
7. ___ rhetoric (n.)	e.	to finalize a business agreement
8. ___ predominant (adj.)	f.	the science of persuasion
9. ___ to inspire (v.)	g.	to motivate someone
	h.	prevailing
	i.	to give supporting arguments

Check your answers on page 151.

Vocabulary Exercise 2—Using the Words in Context

Fill in the blanks with the vocabulary words listed.

close a sale/deal	logical	pros and cons
contend	predominantly	rhetoric
inspire		

1. I tried to reason with him; but his thinking wasn't _____, it was irrational!

2. One needs to consider carefully the _____ of taking an overseas assignment before making such a big move.

3. When I was little, my mother usually tried to _____ with me; when that failed, she threatened me with punishment.

4. I _____ that I am responsible and experienced enough for my boss to trust me with the next major project.

5. What I learned in my class in _____ helped me persuade the interviewer to hire me.

6. This client keeps changing his mind; I don't think I'll ever _____ .

7. Enthusiasm figured _____ in everything he did—that is the secret to his success.

8. Because of Stephan's ability to _____ his employees to work hard for the company, he was given a promotion and a raise.

Check your answers on page 151.

The purpose of your presentation determines the type of rhetoric to use in your presentation. If you are explaining a new procedure, you are being informative; if you are trying to make a sale, you are persuading; if you want to encourage your coworkers to make a deadline, you are inspiring; if you are trying to make a deal and sign a contract, you are negotiating.

Most presentations include some of all of these styles of rhetoric. That is, most communication includes a little information, a little persuasion, and a little inspiration, but one of these types of rhetoric will be the predominant tone of your presentation.

In informational presentations, you are mostly giving facts, without a lot of emotional input. The purpose of an inspirational presentation, however, is to move the audience emotionally, usually to give them encouragement or hope or some other positive feeling that will lead them to take action. Persuasion involves both the rational side and the emotional side. Experienced salespeople tell us that people make a decision to buy based on their emotions and then come up with rational reasons to support their decision. Never underestimate the need for both rational and emotional arguments!

Think about It!

1. In pairs or groups, brainstorm about the variations in information, language, and technique used in informational, inspirational, and persuasive presentations.

2. Commercials and advertisements are designed to persuade you to purchase a product or service. Watch several commercials and look at several print ads. Notice the ways that advertisements attempt to persuade you. How do they use color, words, images, sound, and silence to make rational and emotional arguments? Some commercials and ads are full of information. Are they, nevertheless, persuasive? In what way?

3. Plan a short presentation in which you inform your audience about a new project your company is undertaking or a new product you would like to sell or about any other information you would like to present. Notice when you stop being informative and start being persuasive—it can be a very fine line. Often, during the question-and-answer period of a presentation, you will find yourself being persuasive as well as informative.

4. Plan a short presentation in which you inspire your audience to do, act, be, or feel a certain way. Notice your use of both information and persuasion when being inspirational. What inspires you? Can you do the same for your audience? How do you have to modify what you would do for yourself to fit your audience?

5. Brainstorm with your classmates or a friend about the difference between blatant persuasion and subtle persuasion. What is the difference between persuasion by arguing and convincing and persuasion by suggesting and hinting? Which persuades you more successfully—a head on and up front approach or subtle seduction?

PRESENTATION EXERCISE

Make a presentation in which you convince your audience to marry you. Do not *inform* us about what a good husband or wife is—*persuade* us to marry you. Be sure to give both rational and emotional reasons. Be both persuasive and inspiring.

This is not as easy as it sounds! But it will help you clarify and understand the differences among persuading, informing, and inspiring. It will also make clear the importance of using both rational and emotional arguments. Don't forget to have fun!

OBSERVE AND GIVE FEEDBACK

Observe a persuasive presentation. If you are in a class, watch your classmates' presentations in which they try to persuade you to marry them. Did they use both rational and emotional reasons? Did they argue persuasively? Were you willing to say yes? Why or why not? Use the Presentation Evaluation Form in appendix E (p. 147) for feedback.

CROSS-CULTURAL ISSUES

The kind of information that is considered to be acceptable supporting information varies from culture to culture, as does the kind of logic used, the use of emotions, morality, and other issues. For example, businesspeople from the United States like to see facts and figures, even if the numbers are projected, but the Japanese do not consider projected estimates to be hard, reliable data.

In some cultures, such as in the United States, decisions may be made by a representative of the company, whereas in other cultures, such as Japan or Mexico, the representative may have to take the information back to a superior who will then make the decision. In some cultures, consensus decision making is the norm, whereas in others, everyone votes, and, in still others, decisions are made by authority figures.

Some cultures, such as in Somalia, find stories and proverbs completely convincing, because the people reason analogically to the connection with the current situation. In other cultures, analogies are suspect because no two situations are perfectly parallel.

For some cultures, the prestige of the speaker can carry more weight than the message and arguments themselves. This can be true in Mexico, some of the NIS countries, and very many local settings.

For more information on persuasion, see appendix D, "Persuasion as Cross-Cultural Communication," (p. 145).

Chapter 7

Organizing Your Material, or How to Say What You Want to Say

You may have a wealth of vital information, but if it is not organized in a meaningful way, your audience may become inattentive, confused, frustrated, or even angry. You want to be clearly understood, effective in communicating, and convincing in your reliability to speak on your topic.

FIRST THINGS FIRST

Your closing will summarize your main idea or goal, so start there, at the close, and work backward. Go next to the introduction and work forward. Work on the body, the middle part, last.

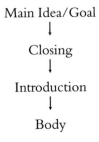

Main Idea/Goal
↓
Closing
↓
Introduction
↓
Body

The first thing you must do is decide what is

the main idea,

the one thought,

the major concept,

the most important thing you want to get across

to your audience. What do you want your audience to understand, to do, to buy, to feel? If you don't have a clear idea of what you want to say, you will not be able to figure out how to say it. You get your main idea from your focus.

Start with the Close!

Once you know what you want to communicate, plan your **closing**—the last section of your presentation. Although you may not be expecting to work on the closing at the beginning, this is the most focused way to proceed. Here's why: the closing is the most important part of your presentation, the last opportunity to say anything to your audience, and it will be the thing they remember most because they heard it last. In your closing, you will review the main idea you want to communicate (in an informational presentation) or make a final convincing argument (in a persuasive one) or tell one last compelling fact or story (in an inspirational one). You may put out a call for action, or make a recommendation, or issue a challenge, or try to close your deal—all of this is in your closing.

Then Work on the Introduction

When you know what you will talk about in your closing, you can turn to the beginning, the **introduction,** and plan how to get to the closing, just as you plan a trip by first deciding what destination you are heading for and then planning the route and means of travel to take to get there.

Your introduction is the second most important part of your presentation. It sets the audience up to hear your closing. A good introduction makes clear your topic (what you are going to talk about), and gives any necessary background that your audience needs to understand your presentation. Sometimes the introduction includes your plan of development, that is, how you are going to get to your destination, the closing.

Most important of all, you want your introduction to grab your audience's attention and get them interested in your presentation. There are several techniques for writing a stimulating introduction.

- Tell a story.

- Cite a quotation from a famous person or well-known book.

- Mention a current or historical event.

- Quote a proverb.

- Tell a joke (in some cultures, not in others).

Whatever grabber you use, it must be *relevant to your topic.* Whichever technique you use, make sure that your opening prepares your audience to hear about your topic and prepares them for your conclusion.

Work on the Body Last

The **body** of your presentation is where you present your ideas, your information, your evidence, and your reasons. Make sure that your ideas are well supported; that is, in the body of the presentation, give the audience additional information that convinces them that your ideas are correct. What is considered to be convincing evidence is different from culture to culture, so be sure you know the cultural values of the people you are speaking to. Don't forget to anticipate and deal with any opposition that someone may have to your ideas. That is, if you suspect that someone in your audience will disagree with one of your points and will have an argument against your point, mention that argument and show how it is wrong. *This last point is critical!*

PUTTING IT ALL TOGETHER

Develop Transitions

Now that you have the rough outline of your three sections (introduction, body, conclusion), think about how to **tie them together,** both conceptually and linguistically. Make connections between ideas, and **transitions** between sentences, that show the relationship between each. If there is a causal relationship, for instance, make it clear that there is a causal relationship. If you are drawing a conclusion based on previously stated information, make that clear.

Signpost for Your Audience

Help your audience follow the structure of your presentation by telling them when you change to a different topic, section, argument, or perspective. This is sometimes called *signposting* because the speaker posts a verbal sign to help the audience follow the train of thought in the presentation.

Remember that, in English, a good rule of thumb is to have one idea per paragraph (or section of your presentation), with all the sentences in that paragraph (or section) speaking to the one idea. When you change ideas, change paragraphs (sections)!

WORD BANK

smooth transition (np.)	an easy move from one thing to another
well- or poorly-organized (adj. cmpd.)	in clear, or confusing, order
signposting (n.)	telling your audience when you are moving on to another topic
to set your audience up for something (idiom)	to prepare them for something you are about to tell them
chronological order (np.)	organized according to the flow of time
summary (n.), to summarize (v.)	a condensed version; to review the main points
thesis (n.)	a proposition or conclusion to be defended in a speech or writing

Read the following sentences that show the Word Bank items used in context. Then do the vocabulary exercise following the sentences to check your comprehension.

1. When the boss was promoted and a new one hired, everyone worked hard to make a *smooth transition* from the old system to the new.

2. a. It didn't matter whether the plan was *well organized* or not; the resistance from the people ensured that it would fail.
   b. Because the department's records were so *poorly organized,* the audit took twice as long.

3. *Signposting* is important in a presentation so that the people can tell where the speaker is going with his or her ideas and when a move is being made.

4. The lighthearted music at the beginning of the movie didn't *set the audience up* for the tragic ending.

What Your Dictionary May Not Tell You!

A note on meaning
To set someone up can also have a negative connotation. It can mean to lie to someone in order to cheat him or her.

5. He described his work history in *chronological order,* starting at the beginning and ending with his retirement.

6. a. The *summary* was a concise abridgment of the long article.
   b. The traveler *summarized* his experiences in a short paragraph.

7. A *thesis* requires proof to be accepted as a conclusion.

Vocabulary Exercise—Using the Words in a Paragraph

Write a paragraph on how to organize a presentation in which you use all the vocabulary words from the Word Bank in one coherent whole.

Spelling Exercise—Hyphenation of Compound Adjectives

Rule: Compound adjectives (two words put together to modify a noun) with *well, better, best, ill, less, little,* and related comparative forms are hyphenated when they come before the noun. Predicate adjectives (when the two words follow the noun) are not hyphenated. Look at the following examples.

- The trade show was *well organized.* (Predicate adjective, no hyphen)

- It was a *well-organized* trade show. (Compound adjective, with hyphen)

Note: Compounds consisting of an *-ly* adverb plus another word are not hyphenated (e.g., poorly planned, badly designed).

In this exercise, show whether the following are compound adjectives or predicate adjectives. Add a hyphen in the space given if they are compound adjectives; if they are predicate adjectives, leave it blank.

1. It was a well ___ known fact that the department head, though tough ___ minded in business situations, volunteered time on his weekends to a youth organization, where he was known to be very soft ___ hearted.
2. He was well ___ known inside and outside of business as a person who cared about the community.
3. John Reynolds was the best ___ paid chief executive officer (CEO) in the company's history.
4. Of all the accountants, André was the best ___ paid.
5. The merger proved to have been ill ___ advised.
6. That ill ___ advised sales idea cost us over a month's revenues.

Check your answers on page 151.

LANGUAGE SUGGESTIONS

The following phrases can help you signal the structure of your presentation to your audience and signpost to them your transitions. Note that most of these are somewhat formal.

1. Signposting

   - First . . . , Second . . . , Next . . . , Last of all . . .

   - I'll begin by . . . , I'll end with . . . , In conclusion . . .

   - I'll be developing . . .

   - My speech will be divided into . . .

   - If I could turn to . . . , My next point . . . , Now, what about . . . , Now, let's look at . . . , Let's move on to . . .

   - So, that's the general picture. Here are the specifics . . .

2. Summarizing

   - Before moving on to the next point, let me review . . .

   - That completes my overview . . .

   - Briefly, what I just said was . . .

3. Showing additional arguments

- In addition, . . .

- Not only . . . but also . . .

- Plus . . .

- . . . And, too, . . .

- Moreover . . .

4. Showing a different argument

- However, . . .

- On the other hand, . . .

- In spite of this . . .

- Let's look at all sides of this issue . . .

5. Showing causes and consequences

- Therefore, . . .

- As a result . . .

- Because of this . . .

- The reason for this is . . .

- Because . . .

- The consequences of this are . . .

ORGANIZATION EXERCISE

This exercise will help you organize your presentation by recognizing signposting and other contextual clues. The following paragraphs that are from a presentation have been scrambled. Put them in order and indicate their order in the presentation by writing the number of the paragraph in the space given. Circle the transition words. Be prepared to discuss the contextual clues that helped you put them into order.

Setting: an informal, in-house meeting

___ So, we've decided to go with CanTool. They are already tooled up to market in this area, with a solid distribution network all over Canada and in several European countries (the U.K., France, Germany, Poland, and the Czech Republic).

___ As you know, although our company is only five years old, growth has been both strong and steady. As a result, we decided to look into a joint venture as a means of expansion. So, we looked into the possibility of working with a French company, a Canadian company, and a Romanian company.

___ We're going into this big-time. We hope to have three new production plants going within six months. Charlie, that's your baby. Take anyone you want from Engineering to work on that. Your contact at CanTool is John Hastings. Susan, your department will be working with Larry McDougal. We want to have another two plants up and running by four months after the first three.

___ Briefly, because of changing regulations in the E.U., we've decided to hold off on working with the French. Although we're keeping the door open for a possibility in the future. In the case of the Romanians, they are not yet up to ISO9000 standards. They'll let us know when they are—they're working on it, but we're not holding our breath.

___ We expect to learn a lot from CanTool's experience in this area, and they're eager to work with us and expand on what they're doing. This is gonna be a lot of work, but we expect it all to be very much worth it. Any questions?

___ And then, we'll be forming a joint marketing team with members from our marketing department and some of theirs. But we're relying heavily on their experience and expertise in this area. Distribution we're leaving entirely to them.

Now, check your organization on page 152.

CROSS-CULTURAL ISSUES

Different cultures organize information in different ways. For instance, some groups and some people prefer deductive thinking (starting with the principle and going to the details); others prefer inductive thinking (starting with the details and going to a conclusion). Europeans tend to analyze, which means to break the information down into parts, but east Asians tend to synthesize, putting the pieces of the puzzle together into a whole.

Germans tend to like things in chronological order; Canadians like to have the recommendations up front, followed by the reasons for the recommendations; the French usually like you to start with a principle or concept and work from that, always referring back to the principle.

All cultures are sometimes direct and sometimes indirect: you need to know which occasions call for a direct approach and which for an indirect approach for the culture you are presenting to. You need to understand how the people tend to think in the culture you will be presenting to so you can organize your information appropriately.

Note: An important point to remember about cultural influences is that psychology is stronger than sociology. That is, individuals often do not conform to the general patterns of their culture but follow their own mix of values.

Now It's Your Turn

How does the organization of information tend to work in your culture? How does it work for you personally? Are you like the majority of people in your culture?

PRESENTATION EXERCISE

Prepare a presentation about a problem and its solution in which you present information in chronological order. Then prepare it again with the recommendations up front, followed by the justification. Pay attention to the changes you have to make in transition language and anything else.

OBSERVE AND GIVE FEEDBACK

Watch a presentation by one of your classmates or by a local politician or on a video from the library and evaluate it in terms of organization. Was the presentation clear and easy to follow? Did the speaker take the listeners along by signposting? Was it appropriate for the culture of the listeners? Make a copy of the Presentation Evaluation Form in appendix E (p. 147) and use it for feedback.

Chapter 8
Crafting and Using Your Notes

A very formal speech may sometimes be read word for word, but, in all other cases, a presentation should not be read. One reason is that few people are trained well enough in the theatrical craft of reading aloud to do a good job of it. They usually read either too fast or in a monotone, hiding their faces and voices in their text, not making themselves understood and boring their audience. Another reason is that written language is more dense and complicated than spoken language, and it is hard for an audience to follow when listening to something that was intended to be read. A third reason is that reading *to* your audience is not the same as communicating *with* them.

Your goals as a presenter are to know thoroughly what you want to communicate, to use notes only as a reminder, and to have give-and-take with your audience.

Tips for Getting Your Audience Involved

Look at them (instead of at your notes!). Observe them, be open to them, be responsive to them. If you can tell they are unclear about a point, stop and explain. Ask them rhetorical questions to keep them thinking about what you are saying. Draw their attention to your visual aids or their handouts. Have them raise their hands in response to a question.

Different people write their notes in different ways. Some write a formal outline, others list their main points on small cards, still others write out ideas with little pictures or other graphic representations to help them remember what they want to say. Some speechmakers write the first few words of each sentence in their notes. Inexperienced presenters sometimes write out complete sentences. But, if you do that, you want to be careful not to end up reading your presentation.

Tips for Making Your Notes Easy to Read

In order to read your notes easily, since you will only be glancing at them occasionally, try these options.

- Print out your notes in large type, so you can see them easily.
- Leave blank space between main ideas.
- Place large color-coded dots beside each section of notes, so your eye will be easily drawn to each section in order.
- Put different sections on different note cards.

Experiment with various kinds of notes and choose the style you like best.

WORD BANK

devising (n.), devise (v.)	invention; to invent
speaking off the cuff (idiom)	speaking without any preparation
spontaneity (n.), spontaneous (adj.), spontaneously (adv.)	action without planning; sudden; unexpectedly, without planning
extemporaneous (adj.), extemporaneously (adv.)	carried out or performed with little or no preparation
impromptu (n., adj.)	arising out of the occasion; not planned; especially of theatrical performances

Read the following sentences that show the Word Bank items used in context. Then do the vocabulary exercise following the sentences to check your comprehension.

1. I don't think he knows what he is talking about; I think he is just speaking *off the cuff.*

2. You may see her behave in unexpected ways because she believes in responding *spontaneously* to life.

3. Press conferences are interesting when they are truly *extemporaneous,* but if the person being interviewed reads a prepared speech, it can be boring.

4. The department head made a long, *impromptu* speech in response to a question about the new project, and so the rest of the agenda was just ignored.

5. He *devised* an ingenious scheme that no one else had ever thought of—and, furthermore, it worked!

Vocabulary Exercise—Expand Your Vocabulary

Fill in the chart with the noun and adverb forms, if the words have these forms.

Noun	*Adjective*	*Adverb*
	spontaneous extemporaneous impromptu	

Check your answers on page 152.

Grammar Exercise 1—Relative Clauses

Relative clause structures can pose a problem for students of English, especially those who speak non-European languages such as Arabic, Hebrew, Chinese, Japanese, Tagalog, and Persian. The following is a brief review covering the most common relative clauses that are used in spoken English.

Keep these simple rules in mind.

1. Relative clauses are "embedded sentences." This means that sentences with relative clauses in them are actually a combination of sentences—one sentence inside another.

2. Relative pronouns *(who, whom, that, which)* replace the noun phrase (NP) in the embedded sentence. The NP is *not* repeated.

3. Choose the relative pronoun according to the following rules.

   • Use *who* to replace a human NP in object or subject position.

     Note: Grammar books tell you to use *whom* for the object case, but this is mostly used in formal writing. Native speakers of American English use *who* almost exclusively in spoken English.

   • Use *which* to replace a nonhuman NP.

   • Use *that* to replace either human or nonhuman NP.

Note: In informal conversational English, *that* is often preferred above *which* and *who(m)*. In written and very formal spoken English, *which* and *who(m)* are preferred. In less formal written English, *that* is often used.

- Use *whose* to show possession. It usually refers to a human head noun but can refer to an inanimate noun.

4. Relative clauses *follow* the NP that they modify.

Tips

Use relative clauses to avoid sounding wordy and redundant. Relative clauses are used a lot by native speakers of English.

I think that this applicant will be more successful than the others. This applicant is a self-starter and he's highly qualified. We should hire him. (relative clause not used)

I think that this applicant, who is a self-starter and highly qualified, will be more successful than the others. We should hire him. (relative clause used)

Do not repeat the noun phrase in the relative clause.
She is *the woman who she* taught me English. (incorrect)
She *is the woman who* taught me English. (correct)

Choose the correct relative pronoun.
John decided to hire the person *which* had a Ph.D. (incorrect)
John decided to hire the person *who* had a Ph.D. (correct)

Position the relative clause after the NP it modifies.
Everyone dislikes *people-biting dogs.* (poor phrasing)
Everyone dislikes *dogs which/that bite people.* (better phrasing)

Think about how relative clauses work in your language. Write down the last sentence in the Tips box as it would be in your language.

Does the relative clause come before or after *dogs?* What is used as a relative pronoun or "marker"?

In English, the relative clause comes after *dogs,* and the relative pronoun is *which* or *that.*

Grammar Exercise 2—Combining Sentences Using Relative Clauses

Look at the examples and then write out the English sentence, combining the two sentences with a relative clause.

Betty said hello to the salesman (she knew the salesman).

Betty said hello to the salesman that/who she knew.

They took the table (the table leaned) away.

They took the table that leaned away.

1. I saw a stain on my tie (the stain upset me).

2. The detective found the gun (the gun was used to kill the victim).

3. Fred Miller is the executive (Fred Miller was promoted to vice president last year).

4. I thought a lot about the raise (I wasn't given a raise).

5. The supervisor gave the worker (the worker was late consistently) a warning.

6. The president looked for the report (his secretary wrote the report).

7. He told the woman (you secretly gave a rose to the woman) all about you.

8. Greg knows about the woman (I hired the woman for the job).

9. I followed the advice (my boss gave me advice).

10. I gave your colleague (you were telling me about your colleague) an article on marketing in France.

11. Dick knew about the problem (his boss was talking about a problem).

12. *The Intelligent Investor* must be the book (you were talking about a book).

Check your answers on page 153.

CROSS-CULTURAL ISSUES

In cultures that are highly oral, such as Somalia, the use of notes should be avoided at all costs. The thinking there is, anyone who needs to rely on notes is not worth listening to. In Taiwan, where academic presentations are usually memorized, using notes can mean that a presenter has not adequately prepared. In the United States, most presenters use notes, but, if they give a good presentation with lots of details without using notes, the audience will be very impressed that the presenter "knows his or her stuff."

Now It's Your Turn

What is it like in your culture? Do people use notes when making presentations? Would the audience be impressed if a person spoke without notes?

GOOD AND BAD EXAMPLES OF NOTES

Sample of bad notes

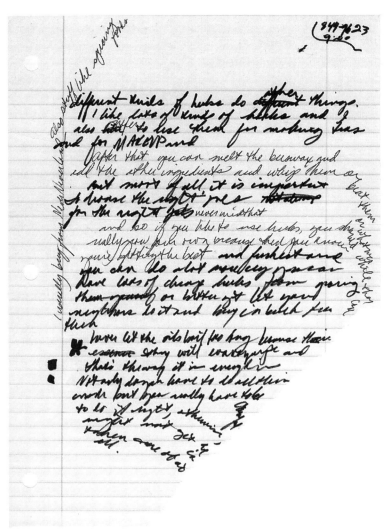

Sample of good notes

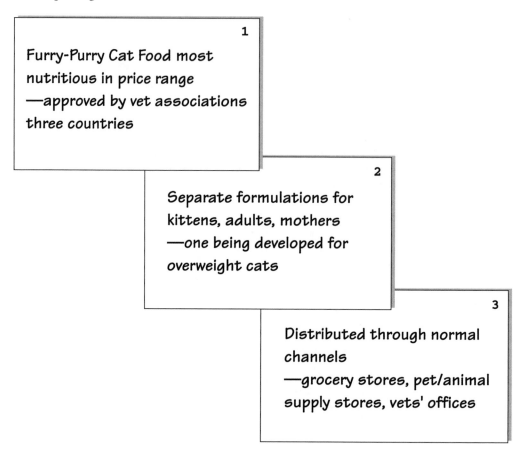

PRESENTATION EXERCISES

Exercise 1

Prepare a short presentation on qualities or characteristics of a good boss or supervisor. Make notes in three different styles, such as 3 × 5 cards, an outline, and another set of your own devising. Decide which one(s) you feel most comfortable using.

Exercise 2

Give the presentation, using your notes. Your focus should be on using your notes well. If you are in a class, have the class fill out the Presentation Evaluation Form in appendix E (p. 147). For self-study, videotape your presentation or have a friend or colleague watch your presentation and use the Presentation Evaluation Form to give you feedback.

OBSERVE AND GIVE FEEDBACK

Watch a presentation. Evaluate the presentation for the use of notes. Did the presenter use notes? Did the presenter read the notes or refer to them occasionally? How did that affect the quality of the presentation? That is, how did the speaker's use of notes or a text affect the speech's "listenability"? Did the presenter communicate *with* the audience or talk *at* them? That is, was there give-and-take between the speaker and the audience? What might the speaker have done to draw the audience in more, to get audience involvement?

Chapter 9

Language

Depending on variables such as your audience, the purpose of your presentation, and the time and location of the presentation, you have to modify the language you use.

In general, a presentation requires formal language. However, you may want to be more informal if the situation calls for it—such as, if you are making a speech at the company picnic (where the atmosphere is more relaxed), or before a group of young children (who may not know sophisticated vocabulary), or at a family gathering (where impromptu expressions of familial affection may be in order). If you are in doubt as to how formal the situation should be, ask someone who knows. If you cannot find out ahead of time, it is usually better to err on the side of formality. Watch your audience and respond to them.

If you are speaking before a group of non-native speakers, here are some good tips.

- Avoid idioms, metaphors, and slang.

- Use simple sentence construction.

- Use short sentences (about 16 words).

- Speak in complete sentences.

- Use active, not passive, forms.

- Choose common words (consult a frequency list).

- Choose words with only one meaning; use a word in its most common meaning; be aware that the same word (or phrase) may have a different meaning in a different culture.

- Use redundancy and repetition to clarify and emphasize.

- Define your terms.

If your English is sophisticated enough, consider the language background of your non-native listener. If your audience is from a germanic language background (for

---

The tips are based on suggestions in "Translation Problems in International Marketing Research," by Dennis Guthery and Bonnie A. Lowe, *Journal of Language for International Business* 4, no. 1 (1992): 1–14.

example, if these individuals come from Germany, the Netherlands, Norway, Denmark, England), choose your vocabulary from words of Anglo-Saxon origin. If your audience is from a Romance language background (such as people from France, Spain, Italy, Portugal), use words of Latin origin. A good English dictionary will tell you the linguistic origins of a word. But you may have to go to a library to get a dictionary that does that for you.

WORD BANK

to be in order (idiom)	to be appropriate
redundancy (n.), redundant (adj.)	a repetition; repetitive
discourse (n.), to discourse (v.)	a conversation, a lecture, a written treatise; to converse, to lecture
discourse analysis (np.)	a technical term in linguistics, the study of the structure of discourse (this structure varies from language to language)
cue (n.), to cue (v.)	a signal to begin, enter, or take other course of action; from the theater, where to *cue* means to give the signal for an actor, a musician, or a technician to start

The following sentences show the Word Bank items used in context.

1. "We've gotten a lot of work done this morning. At this point, I think a little lunch would *be in order.* Then we can continue in the afternoon."

2. In the English sentence, "The four businesspeople were waiting for the plane," the plurality is demonstrated in three places: "four," "people," and "were." This *redundancy* does not exist in all languages.

3. "The meeting was, basically, a long, boring *discourse* by Fred on things we already know. What a waste of time!"

4. A *discourse analysis* can explain how the structure and style of writing vary in business letters from different cultures.

5. "I'll talk first. When I finish what I have to say, wait a minute to see what Jones is thinking. If he seems open to the proposition, that's your *cue* to come in with your argument."

CROSS-CULTURAL ISSUES

The level of formality, and the use of language, can vary even within a single nation because there are different cultural groups within a country. A presentation before a group of bankers in New York City will need to be more formal than one before a group of computer employees in California's Silicon Valley, even though both groups are from the United States. An academic discourse before a group of university professors would probably be more formal than a talk given to a group of farmers. The language and vocabulary differ with each group.

Even the role of words and language varies from culture to culture. The Japanese, the Danes, and several Native American Indian tribes are well known for being comfortable with silence, for using silence as communication and even needing silence, while other groups (the United States, West Indies) find silence uncomfortable and often interpret silence negatively. The amount and use of pauses within a conversation vary from language to language, as do the rhythms of, and cues for, turntaking.

Language and the use of emotions are closely linked. People in some cultures, such as Japanese and northern European cultures, tend to believe it is better not to express one's emotions in public or at work. But people in southern European cultures believe it is acceptable to do so. The amount of emotion that gets expressed is reflected in (and reinforced by) the language. The British, who prefer to keep their emotions out of public view, enjoy understatement, for instance. The Italians and French both admire the use of beautiful, elegant language, even in a business context. In the United States, where one expresses less emotion at work than elsewhere, that same language might be criticized as "flowery" or even "show-offy."

Now It's Your Turn

What is the role of silence in your culture? How much emotion is considered appropriate to display in public or at work? Are emotions something to be kept out of decision making, or are they to be included? Why? How does this affect language and communication?

EXAMPLES OF GOOD AND BAD LANGUAGE USE

Think about It!

Why do the following examples demonstrate poor or better use of language with an audience of non-native speakers of English? Discuss this with a classmate or colleague or friend.

Poor: I'm really out in left field here. Can you give me a ballpark figure?

Better: "I have very little information about this situation. Can you give me an estimate of what it might cost?"

Poor: "So, you see, it would be great if—I mean, we could all use, that is, some financial advice. About this project."

Better: "So, we all need more information about financing this project."

GRAMMAR REVIEW—ACTIVE AND PASSIVE VOICE

English sentences are constructed with a subject + verb + object (SVO) pattern. In a sentence with an active construction, the subject of the sentence is the person or thing responsible for the action. The subject is the *agent*—it does the action of the verb. The object of an active sentence is the receiver, not the initiator, of the action. We can call the object of an active sentence the *receiver.*

In a sentence with a passive construction, the *agent* is the object and the *receiver* is the subject. The structure is still SVO, but the subject and object have reversed roles, usually because the object is unknown or unimportant.

If the object is named, it is prefaced with the word *by.* The form of the verb changes in passive sentences. The verb form used is *be + the participle.* So, the structure of a passive sentence is: subject + be + the participle (by object).

Grammar Exercise—Active and Passive Voice

Look at the following example, and then do the exercises.

Active:	*The dog*	*bit*	*the runner.*
	Subject	Verb	Object
	(Agent)		(Receiver)
Passive:	*The runner*	*was bitten*	*by the dog.*
	Subject	Verb	Object
	(Receiver)		(Agent)

Make the following passive statements active.

1. My employees are expected to put in overtime.

2. Thirty dozen roses are sold in my flower shop every day.

3. The banquet hall was decorated by our team in the colors of the company logo.

4. A gold watch is received by everyone when they retire.

5. Honesty is emphasized by the company.

Check your answers on page 153.

A note about the passive: There are appropriate times to use the passive voice. Use the passive when

1. the agent is unknown *(The painting has been destroyed.)*
2. the agent is understood (*Apples are grown in these hills.* Understood agent: farmers)
3. you want to emphasize the receiver or result of the action *(Six houses were destroyed by the flood.)*
4. you do not want to identify the agent (to be tactful, or evasive, for instance). *(An error was made in the budget.)*
5. with certain verbs that take the passive, such as *to be born, to be rumored.*

Some places where the passive voice is commonly used are

- in newspaper reports about wars or conflicts
  Fifty civilians were wounded in the bombing. (to emphasize the result)

- in scientific writing
  An instantaneous reaction is caused when vinegar and baking soda are combined. (to emphasize the result)

- when talking about awards or citations
  The Nobel Peace Prize was announced today. (agent is understood)

- when someone or something is victimized
  IBM was threatened by a hostile takeover attempt. (agent is unknown, or speaker does not want to identify the agent)

- when someone is a patient in medical situations
  He was examined by the doctor. (to emphasize the result)

PRESENTATION EXERCISES

Exercise 1—Informal Presentation

Prepare a short presentation on "My Ideal Job." Tell why you would prefer that job by talking about such details as whether or not you like to work indoors, with people, as a supervisor, with ideas, with things, doing creative work, doing analytical work, working in sales, finance, human resources, and anything else that would explain what your ideal job would be.

Exercise 2—Formal Presentation

Choose a topic of your preference to be presented in a formal situation. Before you present, in groups, or alone, practice your presentation with an awareness of language issues.

- Shorten long sentences.

- Watch your choice of vocabulary.

- Explain any idioms and metaphors that you use.

- Use active constructions, unless you have a good reason to use the passive voice.

OBSERVE AND GIVE FEEDBACK

Watch a classmate's presentation or watch a presentation outside of your classroom. Use the Presentation Evaluation Form in appendix E (p. 147) to evaluate it. Pay special attention to the use of language. Was it appropriate for the audience, for the purpose, and for the occasion? Did the presenter define new terms? Did the presenter use active constructions where possible? Did the presenter avoid unfamiliar idioms and metaphors? Were the sentences too long?

Chapter 10

Technique

Watch a video of or listen to a recorded speech given by one or more of the following speechmakers.

> Nelson Mandela
>
> Martin Luther King Jr.
>
> Margaret Thatcher
>
> Mother Teresa of Calcutta

Think about more intimate speech situations.

> The salesperson who convinced you to buy a recent major purchase
>
> The last excellent presenter you listened to
>
> The teacher in your class

As you look over the preceding list of famous and not-so-famous speakers, try not to think about their message but, rather, about their delivery. A good delivery, made with good technique, can greatly influence how a speaker's presentation is perceived. Great speakers show that they care deeply about their topics and demonstrate their respect for their audiences by, among other things, using good technique. Technique can also help a nervous speaker relax and appear calm and confident.

Voice

- Speak with conviction. If you don't believe what you are saying, neither will your audience.

- Don't speak too fast—think about loving every word that you say.

- Speak loudly enough to be heard in the back of the room.

- If you use a microphone, practice ahead of time so you know how to use it. Test a microphone by tapping it with your finger—never blow into a microphone.

- Vary the volume, tone, and intensity of your speech according to what you are saying.

- Speak with exaggerated articulation. Especially emphasize the consonants, which play a major role in conveying meaning in the English language.

Facial Expression

- Unless we train ourselves otherwise, our faces naturally express what we feel. Let your natural feelings for your ideas show through on your face. Your audience will understand your presentation better as a result of your facial expressions and will probably mirror you with similar emotions or attitudes.

Response to your Audience

- Pay attention to what your audience is doing and respond appropriately. If they are laughing at your humor, pause and enjoy it with them. If it seems that they are having trouble understanding, stop and find out if they are. In most situations, it is appropriate to ask an audience questions and take their verbal response: "Are you following me?" "Am I going too fast?" "Can you hear me in the back?"

Dress Professionally

- Wear clothes that do not distract from your message either visually or audibly.

- Wear subdued jewelry—avoid dangling earrings, pendants, or tie clips; remove large rings and excessive jewelry (with the exception of unobtrusive wedding rings).

- Comb your hair in a neat style that does not hang in your face.

- Iron your clothes.

- Wear understated clothes—not too sexy, trendy, or bright for your audience.

Eye Contact

- Although eye contact varies from culture to culture, in most English-speaking countries, maintaining eye contact is essential.

- Include your entire audience in your eye contact.

- Use your eyes, facial expressions, and gestures to invite your audience to look at you.

Good eye contact   Poor eye contact

Good eye contact includes looking at everyone in the audience. Looking at only one place in the room or down at your notes is not good eye contact.

Tip

If you are presenting to a small group, and you feel uncomfortable with direct eye contact, you can look at the point on the forehead just above and between the eyes. Your audience will still feel that you are looking them in the eyes, and you might not feel so nervous.

EFFECTIVE PAUSES AND EMPHASIS

"Your pause is your most important weapon!"

- Plan your pauses and spoken emphasis.

- Pause after, or repeat, something important or difficult to understand.

- Pause after you have asked a question.

- When you pause, look at your audience.

GESTURES

Every gesture has a purpose, namely, to help express meaning. Gestures come naturally out of what we are trying to communicate. If your gestures look artificial, you are concentrating too hard on the gesture and not on the message you are trying to communicate. Meaningless gestures look like nervous fidgeting and distract the audience. Practice in the mirror before you give your speech.

Movement and Use of Space

- Movements depend on the kind of speech you are giving, the shape of the room and the arrangement of furniture, and the kind of relationship you want to have with your audience.

- Movements that are relaxed and purposeful are best. Artificial movement distracts your audience.

- Moving closer to your audience increases intimacy and intensity. You can do this by walking closer to your audience or by bending over a podium, if you are using one.

- Think about how an actor on a stage uses space and movement. When you are presenting, you are performing.

- You do not have to move, but stand naturally. Stiffness may cause your audience to feel tense.

Posture

- Relaxed, upright posture shows that you are confident about your presentation.

- Keep both feet on the ground at shoulder width. Avoid shifting your weight from one foot to the other.

- Avoid leaning on the podium or table.

- Keep your shoulders back and your arms relaxed.

- Never, ever, slouch.

The key to all of these techniques is that they can help you demonstrate that you care about your topic and respect your audience. Practice, concentrate on your message, and your technique will naturally improve.

Note: Technique can help prevent or lessen nervousness, but many people, even professional actors and speakers, still feel nervous when they have to make a presentation. Your goal is not to stop being nervous but to be able to do a good job even if you are nervous.

Exercise 1—Eye Contact

Place objects or pictures of people about the room. Look at the faces or objects when you practice your speech.

Exercise 2—Voice Projection

If you have trouble projecting your voice, try the following.

1. Bend at the waist and place your hands on either side of your lower back just below your ribs.

2. Breathe deeply until you feel both sides of your back expand.

3. As you breathe out, use that part of your body, the diaphragm, to push out some sounds. You can begin by saying vowel sounds such as "ah, ah, ah. . . ." When your volume is loud enough, stand up straight.

4. Now, in a standing position, with your hands still on your lower back, speak a sentence aloud. Concentrate on using your diaphragm to push the sound out. Try not to use your throat or your lungs to push the sound out.

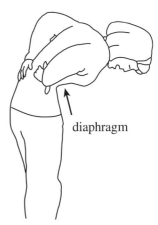

diaphragm

Bending over and putting your hands on your back just above your waist helps you feel yourself breathing from your diaphragm.

People whose speaking voices do not project are generally using their lungs or throats to carry the sound. Professional actors, singers, and speakers use their diaphragms to project their voices. This allows their voices to carry farther with less strain on the throat and vocal cords. Individuals who use their lungs to project their voices tend to become breathless more easily and appear less confident when giving a presentation.

CROSS-CULTURAL ISSUES

The eye contact that a speaker uses varies from culture to culture. In some cultures, maintaining eye contact with your audience is considered rude or even threatening. For example, in Japan, you might offend an older audience by too much eye contact or by expecting them to look directly into your eyes. In contrast, you would have a hard time keeping the attention of a U.S. audience if you did not maintain eye contact throughout your speech. Too much eye contact with one individual, however, will make the entire audience uncomfortable. It is important to ask your hosts about eye contact in their country before giving a presentation.

Now It's Your Turn

In your culture, how much eye contact is expected in a presentation? If you are unsure, observe the next presenter that you hear from your culture. Does the presenter look at the entire audience or at one person in particular? Do you think that the speaker's eye contact is appropriate for the audience? Does it make you feel comfortable or uncomfortable?

PRESENTATION EXERCISE—TECHNIQUE

In this presentation, focus more on technique than on content. Your peer review or your self-analysis will be based on the delivery of your presentation. Use the Presentation Planning Guide (p. 88) to prepare for your speech. Because this speech is focusing on technique, choose a topic with which you are quite familiar, so that you don't have to do any research. The following are some suggestions.

- Tell something about your job.

- Talk about a favorite hobby, holiday, vacation trip.

- Describe your family or a family member, friend, or colleague.

- Convince the audience to buy your product or a product you like.

- Argue for or against some controversial topic, like smoking in public places.

- Pick any topic of your choice.

OBSERVE AND GIVE FEEDBACK

Use the Peer/Self-Evaluation Form on p. 89, and focus only on technique.

WORD BANK

gesture (n.), to gesture (v.)
diaphragm (n.)
trend (n.), trendy (adj.)
to fiddle with (idiom)
fidgets (n.), to fidget (v.), fidgety (adj.)
eulogy (n.)

distraction (n.), to distract (v.), distracting (adj.)
articulation (n.), to articulate (v.), articulate (adj.)
emphasis (n.), to emphasize (v.), emphatic (adj.)
pause (n.), to pause (v.)
delivery (n.), to deliver (v.)

Guess the meanings of the following italicized words from their contexts. Then do the vocabulary exercise following the sentences to check your comprehension.

1. a. Because the construction noise outside was *distracting,* the committee had trouble concentrating on their decision.
   b. His worry about the upcoming move was a serious *distraction* from his work.
   c. While trying to practice, he was *distracted* by the beautiful spring breeze coming in the window.

What Your Dictionary Might Not Tell You!

A note on prepositions
A distraction is distracting *to* someone.
One is distracted *by* something.

---

2. a. At the celebration party, he *delivered* congratulatory speeches with great humor.
   b. If the *delivery* of the presentation is too slow, the audience will get bored; if it is too fast, the audience will get irritated.

3. a. Because of a clear communication style, the speaker was considered an *articulate* person.
   b. An actor must learn to *articulate* his words clearly, in order to be heard and understood in the back row of the theater.
   c. Her *articulation* improved after she went through speech therapy.

   A note on pronunciation
   articulate (adj.) the *a* in the final syllable is pronounced as a schwa /ə/

   articulate (v.) the *a* in the final syllable is pronounced as a long *a* or /e/

4. The Heimlich maneuver involves applying a short, sudden pressure to the *diaphragm* to force out food or anything else that is stuck there.

5. a.   The hand sign that means "okay" in the United States is a vulgar *gesture* in Korea.
   b.   He *gestured* for her to stop by raising his index finger.

What Your Dictionary Might Not Tell You!

A note on prepositions
One gestures *for* someone to do something.

---

6. a.   The long *pause* following the president's speech made his cabinet members nervous.
   b.   She *paused* to catch her breath; then she continued speaking.
   c.   Fred *paused* for a moment to collect his thoughts.

What Your Dictionary Might Not Tell You!

A note on prepositions
One pauses *for* an amount of time.

---

7. Mary disliked spending money every six months to buy her son *trendy* new clothes. She felt that she couldn't afford always to keep up with the latest fads.

8. a.   The *emphasis* in Chuck's first-year English class was on reading; the *emphasis* in his second-year class was on writing.
   b.   Cynthia's boss *emphasized* quality over quantity. He expected her to spend enough time to do a good job.

9. When Jorge was nervous, he *fiddled with* his keys. Even such a small movement made a lot of noise.

10. a. Olga's smooth, easy, relaxed movements contrasted sharply with Valentine's *fidgety* ones.
    b. Waiting to hear the election results, the nervous candidate started to *fidget*.

11. At the funeral, he gave the *eulogy* with controlled emotion.

Vocabulary Exercise—Crossword Puzzle

You will find some of the answers to this crossword puzzle in the preceding Word Bank. Others appear in the chapter text.

Across

1. If a word is important in a speech, then __ it.
3. Use your __, instead of your throat and lungs, to speak louder.
5. Dangly earrings and shiny rings are __ to an audience.
8. The __ in this chapter is technique.
9. In order to have good __, you have to look at your entire audience. Don't look at one person only or bury your eyes in your notes. (two words)
10. He didn't use __. He kept his arms stiffly at his sides.

Down

2. When you __ your words, it is easier to understand your speech.
4. Don't __ with your pen. When you move it around like that it's distracting.
6. His __ was terrible. He shifted his weight from foot to foot.
7. __ clothes are distracting.

Check your answers on page 153.

Presentation Planning Guide

Before you begin, follow these suggestions for preparation.

- Practice your speech in front of a mirror. Refer back to the "Eye Contact," "Gestures," "Movement and Use of Space," and "Posture" sections for tips.
- Tape-record your speech and listen to it critically, keeping in mind the suggestions in the "Effective Pauses and Emphasis" and "Voice" sections.
- What are you wearing? Is it neat and nondistracting?

Speech

- Look at your entire audience.
- Speak loudly enough to be heard.
- Speak slowly and clearly.
- Be careful not to use any nervous gestures. Don't hold a pencil, pen, or any other object that will end up distracting your audience.
- If you move, be sure that you have planned it.
- Relax your posture.

Make copies of the Peer/Self-Evaluation form as needed.

Peer/Self-Evaluation Form

On a scale of one to five, with one lowest and five highest, rate yourself and your colleagues on technique.

Dress (distracting? neat?)	1	2	3	4	5
Voice (spoke with conviction? loud enough? easy to understand?)	1	2	3	4	5
Eye contact (did it include the entire audience?)	1	2	3	4	5
Facial expression (varied and meaningful?)	1	2	3	4	5
Pauses and emphasis (were they effective?)	1	2	3	4	5
Gestures (did they look natural?)	1	2	3	4	5
Movement (was it appropriate?)	1	2	3	4	5
Posture (was it relaxed, yet upright?)	1	2	3	4	5

Overall comments:

This form is reproducible.

Chapter 11

Visual Aids

WORD BANK

clutter (n.), to clutter (v.)   right here (idiom)   retention (n.), to retain (v.)
to gravitate (v.)   right now (idiom)   retainer fee (np.)

Guess the meanings of the following italicized words from their contexts. Then do the vocabulary exercise following the sentences to check yourself.

1. a.   This room is a mess! Clear away this *clutter* on the table.
   b.   The waiting room was *cluttered* with empty coffee cups and dirty ashtrays.

2. His eyes continually *gravitated* to the impressive view out the window—he couldn't keep his eyes from it.

3. a.   "The digging will start *right here,*" Tomlinson said, pointing to the ground, "and continue to the end of the block."
   b.   You'll be doing your presentation *right here,* where we are standing.

4. a.   Hurry! The tour is starting *right now!*
   b.   *Alfredo:* "It's 4 o'clock. What time does the meeting start?"
   c.   *Paolo:* "Four o'clock. Yikes! That's *right now.*"

5. a.   His memory *retention* was incredible. He met 50 people from the other firm at one meeting and remembered everyone's name and where they worked.
   b.   We want to *retain* the copyright to this new software.
   c.   I can call my lawyer any time I need him—he is well worth his *retainer fee.*

Vocabulary Exercise—Definitions

Write what you think the words mean in the spaces provided.

clutter (n.) _____ to clutter (v.) _____

right here (idiom) _____ right now (idiom) _____

to gravitate (v.) _____

retention (n.) ————————————— to retain (v.) —————————————

retainer fee (np.) ————————————————————————————

Check your answers on page 154.

Use visual aids to help your audience understand and remember what you are saying. The more simple a visual aid is, the easier it is to understand and remember. The rule for designing visual aids is, "One idea, one visual!"

When you prepare your visual aids, it is a good idea to think of traffic signs. An effective traffic sign is clear, easy to read from a distance, and limited to one message.

Visual aids make a big difference in how your audience responds to your presentation. Research on visual aids shows the following.

With visual aids
- your audience is 43% more likely to be persuaded
- customers or clients will pay 26% more money for the same product or service
- learning is improved 200%
- retention is improved 38%
- time to explain complex subjects is reduced by 25–40%
- the presenter is perceived as more professional, more credible, more persuasive, and better prepared.

———————————

Information on visual aids reported by David Peoples in *Presentations Plus* (New York: John Wiley and Sons, 1992), 3–6.

There are many more options for visual aids available to presenters today than in the past. They range from the most simple to the technologically advanced. The following is a list of some of the most common.

- Chalkboards or whiteboards

- Flip charts (large pads of paper that are supported by easels)

- Poster board (large pieces of thin, colored cardboard)

- Handouts

- Overhead projectors (OHPs)

- Slide projectors and slides

- Videos

- Computers with overhead capabilities

- Presentation software

You can make your visual aids yourself using this equipment or hire graphics professionals to make them for you. Appendix B, "Additional Resources," on page 141 lists companies that manufacture equipment for making presentations.

Choose the simplest option that is appropriate for your situation. Sophisticated technology is not necessarily the most appropriate; sometimes the simple solution is the best. Let your presentation determine your visual aids; your visual aids should not drive your presentation.

Tips for Preparing Visual Aids Using Any Materials or Technology

1. Avoid clutter. Visual aids should support your presentation, not detract from it.
2. Keep the message clear and simple.
3. Make the visual aids attractive, neat, and well prepared, with a professional look.
4. Make the visual aids large enough to be seen by the entire audience.
5. Design the visual aid so that the audience's eyes will gravitate to what you want to emphasize.
6. Use color to increase your audience's attention span by 85%.
7. Use no more than three colors per visual, so as not to distract your audience.
8. One idea, one visual aid

EXAMPLES OF GOOD AND BAD VISUAL AID STRUCTURES

Using the preceding tips, explain why this is a good visual aid.

Best New Market

    for *Golden Years* line

             MEN

             urban

             50+

Using the preceding tips, look at the following three visual aids and decide what is wrong with each.

1. Furry-Purry Cat Food is the most nutritious cat food available in its price range. It has been approved by veterinarian associations in three countries and is recommended by the Cat Breeders Association. There are separate formulations for kittens, adult cats, and mother cats, and a further formulation is being developed for overweight cats. The basic formulation contains chicken, wheat, ground corn, ground brown rice, whole soybeans, dried kelp, taurine, zinc, and vitamins A, B, and D. The amount fed should be adjusted to maintain ideal body weight. Furry-Purry Cat Food is sold in three sizes of bags, just as our Fuzzy-Wuzzy Dog Food is. Distribution is through normal channels—grocery stores, pet and animal supply stores, and veterinarian's offices.

2.

Furry-Purry Sales are Going up

3.

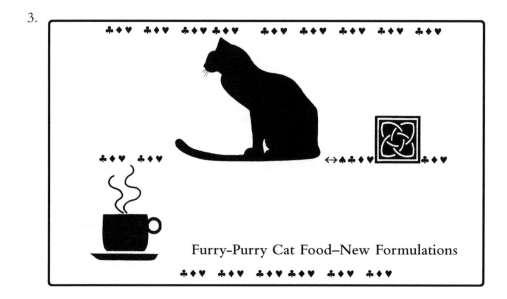

Furry-Purry Cat Food–New Formulations

You can design better visual aids by correcting the mistakes in the three preceding items. Take one idea from the information in the first visual aid on Furry-Purry Cat Food and make a good visual aid in the box on page 95. Refer to the Tips for Preparing Visual Aids Using Any Materials or Technology on page 92.

1.

Not all visual aids are alike. The following are notes for specific types of visuals.

1. Computer or overhead projector (OHP)

   • Enlarge the print or font before you use it. Put less on a screen or trans-parency, rather than more. Your audience needs to be able to see your visual aid clearly and grasp it instantly. Save space by using fewer words, not a smaller font!

   • Bring a backup lightbulb for the OHP and a surge protector if you are using a computer.

2. Slides

   • Preview all slides before making the presentation. Few things are more em-barrassing in a presentation than a misplaced or upside-down slide.

   • Focus the projector on the first slide before the audience arrives.

   • Take a backup lightbulb.

3. Video

- Make sure that you know how to run the VCR before your presentation.

- Before the presentation, set the video to the beginning of the segment you want to show.

- Adjust the volume and tracking before the audience arrives.

- Ensure that the television screen is at a proper level and positioned so that the entire audience can see it comfortably.

- Use short video clips (short segments of the video) and don't let it run too long. A general rule of thumb is no more than three minutes.

4. Chalkboard or marker board

- Bring your own chalk, dry erase markers, erasers, and a damp rag.

- Use a variety of colors to make your message stand out.

5. Flip chart

- Take your own easel, flip chart, and pens.

- Make sure that the easel is stable.

- Plan your movements so that you don't trip over the easel.

- The pages can be torn off and hung on the wall for later reference.

- This is one of the easiest visual aids to use; little can go wrong.

6. Handouts. Here are some different ways to use handouts.

- Include information that you don't have time to present.

- Provide an outline that the audience can use to organize their notes.

- Give the audience something to walk away with—your major points.

- Supply your audience with a bibliography for further reading.

USING VISUAL AIDS

Place the visuals so that your audience can easily glance from you to the visual aid and back again. Do not block your visual. If you are writing or drawing on the visual, such as on a chalkboard or flip chart, do not turn your back to your audience and speak into the visual—turn toward your audience before you start speaking again.

Prepare your audience for the visual aid, especially if you are going to show a video clip. Explain the visual, interpret it, comment on it. Give additional information that is not on the visual aid.

It is often a good idea to display a visual aid for the audience to look at when they first arrive in the room. You can have basic identification, such as your company's logo, your name, and the name of your presentation on the visual. Another option is to put up questions or information related to the presentation that will get your audience thinking about the topic.

During the presentation, leave a visual aid in sight until you move on to your next point. Another option is, when you are finished with a visual aid, replace it with a generic title page (such as the one with identification on it) or replace it with the visual that introduced this section of your presentation.

CROSS-CULTURAL ISSUES

Be careful in your use of colors if you are presenting in a culture unfamiliar to you. Using large red letters on white paper or writing someone's name and including his or her picture on a visual aid can produce a visual that looks like a funeral banner in Chinese-speaking countries.

Symbols and graphics can also be dangerous. The hand sign that means *okay* to people in English-speaking countries (the thumb and forefinger touching to form an *O*) is a vulgar gesture in Korea and some other countries; and crossing your fingers—a sign of wishing good luck in the United States—is obscene in Vietnam. In Japan and China, the number four sounds like the word for death and therefore symbolizes death. The number 13 signifies bad luck in most Christian countries. It's a good idea to check with your host to find out whether there are any taboo color combinations, numbers, or symbols.

Now It's Your Turn

Are there any numbers, colors, or other symbols that are inappropriate to use in your country?

Learning Styles. Some learners are visually oriented and need to have something to look at in order to learn. Among those, some are visually-verbally oriented and therefore need words in their visual aids, and some are visually-pictorially oriented and, as a result, need pictures. Handouts give tactile learners an object to hold and to take notes on, thus helping them learn according to their natural learning style. Asking your audience to do something with their bodies, such as raising their hands, writing something down, or moving around the room, helps bodily kinesthetic learners to stay focused and retain what they are learning.

PRESENTATION EXERCISE

Make Your Own Visual Aids

1. Choose from the different types of visual aid materials and plan a presentation in which you own a flower shop and are convincing other shop owners to join in buying a refrigerated truck for delivering flowers around three major cities in your area. Include at least one visual aid that uses statistics (number of deliveries per day, comparison of amounts of different flowers delivered, etc.). You may use invented statistics for this presentation. Use the checklist that follows. Or choose your own topic. Include at least two visual aids, one of which uses statistics. You may use invented statistics for this presentation. Use the checklist that follows.

Visual Aids Checklist

__ Is there only one idea per visual aid?
__ Is the idea of each visual aid clear and instantly grasped?
__ Do the visual aids look professional (neat and easy to read)?
__ Are they the appropriate size for the room and the audience (not too large, not too small)?
__ Are they colorful?

---

2. Think about how you would change these visual aids for a different kind of material. For example, if you used a flip chart, how would you modify the visual to turn it into an overhead? And so on.

Note: Making effective visual aids takes a lot of practice!

3. Give your presentation, using whichever set of visual aids you prefer. Ideally, videotape yourself.

OBSERVE AND GIVE FEEDBACK

Watch your classmates' presentations and your own or some other local presentation, paying close attention to the use of visual aids. Use the preceding checklist and the Presentation Evaluation Form in appendix E (p. 147).

Listen to radio advertisements and watch television advertisements. Notice the differences between the two. Television has visual aids! Which influences you more? How do radio advertisements try to help you make pictures in your mind?

Chapter 12

Planning for Last-Minute Changes and Disasters

Murphy's Law: If it can go wrong, it will!

No matter how well prepared you are, or how experienced you are, last-minute changes or problems may arise. Be ready to deal with them!

DISASTERS

What if you arrived at your presentation destination and discovered that there was no blackboard or that the whiteboard was missing its markers? Or, just as you began your presentation, the lightbulb in the overhead projector blew? And the second projector they brought in also didn't work?

You want to be as prepared as possible for these kinds of problems. Ideally, you will carry with you all the equipment you need—including extra extension cords and lightbulbs; markers, erasers, and cleaners; blank transparencies; chart paper, and so on.

This is easy in the case of whiteboard markers but more difficult with overhead projectors. If you had to, could you give your presentation without using a chalkboard or the overhead? Do you have handouts that would provide the same information that you planned to put on the overhead? What if the airline lost your luggage, including all your handouts and your notes?

UNEXPECTED CHANGES

What would you do if you got there and found that the audience was twice (or half) the size you expected? Or that they wanted to hear a different perspective on your topic from what you had planned? Or that they wanted to use a translator? Or all three? How about if the plane was delayed and you arrived with only 15 minutes of your presentation time remaining?

No need to panic! Here are some ideas for handling these difficult situations.

Tips for Avoiding Disasters

1. Get as much information as possible from people on-site regarding the audience, location, and facilities.
2. Have a backup plan for all aspects of your presentation.
3. If you are not sure of the facilities, plan to use handouts or a flip chart that you can carry yourself.
4. Never check essentials (handouts, notes, clothes) with the airline; if you can't carry all of your handouts onto the plane with you, then carry the originals. Copies can be made at the site, if necessary.

Tips for Dealing with Disasters

1. Don't get too attached to a particular technology or technique; you need to be able to modify and simplify things, often at the last minute.
2. Take extra material, in case there is extra time (for whatever reason!). It is better to have too much than too little.
3. Take a backup system for your visual aids. If you plan to use an overhead projector, consider how your visuals could be modified to another medium, such as a chalkboard.
4. Take control of the situation to improve things. For instance, if the audience turns out to be smaller than anticipated and spread out over a large room, ask them to come to the front and sit close together. Turn your grand lecture into a cozy discussion, if possible.

Exercise—Modifying Your Presentation

Think about the kinds of modifications you would have to make in a presentation under the following conditions. Think in terms of content, presentation style, visual aids, activities, and anything else that is relevant. If you are in a class, discuss this in groups.

a. The audience was one-fourth the size you expected.
b. The presentation was supposed to last one-third longer than you expected.
c. You needed an open room for an activity, and the room was full of chairs bolted to the floor.
d. The audience had no background in your topic (you thought they were going to be experienced in the field).
e. You came prepared to sell your audience on a product and found they needed to be trained to sell it themselves.

WORD BANK

to deal with (idiom)
to cope with (idiom)
panic (n.), to panic (v.), panicky (adj.)

flexibility (n.), to be flexible (vp.), flexible (adj.)
backup (n. & adj.), to back up (v.)

Guess the meanings of the following italicized words from their contexts. Then do the vocabulary exercise following the sentences to check yourself.

1. How are we going *to deal with* this new problem, so that we can get it solved by the deadline?

2. Maria is pretty good at *coping with* difficult situations; we always give her the tricky problems in our department.

3. a. Job interviews always send Susan into a *panic,* and her nervousness comes across as incompetence.
   b. Don't send John to do delicate negotiations—if something goes wrong, he *panics* and makes irrational decisions.
   c. Don't get *panicky!* If you remain calm, we can take care of this problem easily and quickly.

4. a. *Flexibility* is built into this plan, because we don't know what changes may have to be made.

b. When choosing someone for an overseas assignment, I want a *flexible* person who can adapt to different situations.

c. Oak trees don't bend in the wind, and Laila isn't very *flexible,* either—no matter what the situation is.

5. a. It is important to think about what your alternate, or *backup,* plan will be.

b. I'm *backing up* my files now, so that, in case anything goes wrong with the hard drive, I'll have copies.

Vocabulary Exercise—Matching Synonyms and Antonyms

Now that you have made an educated guess about the meanings of the words, fill in the chart. Choose from the following words: calm, rigid, pliable, substitute, hysterical, sole

Word	*Synonym*	*Antonym*
flexible backup panicky		

Check your answers on p. 154.

Can you think of some more synonyms and antonyms? Try your dictionary and thesaurus.

GOOD AND BAD RESPONSES TO LAST-MINUTE CHANGES OR DISASTERS

Bad Responses

Freeze with terror.

Refuse to go on.

Ignore the need for modification and deliver your presentation as planned.

Good Responses

Remain calm.

Take charge.

Do what needs to be done quickly, calmly, and efficiently.

Get help to make any necessary changes.

Delegate any work that you can.

Maintain a good sense of humor.

Be gracious.

CROSS-CULTURAL ISSUES

Some cultures are relaxed about problems and delays. Other cultures expect you to do whatever it takes to solve the problem—immediately! If you are making a presentation in the former, you need to be relaxed and accepting of limitations. If you are presenting in the latter, you need to be prepared to act quickly and sometimes very inventively to solve the problem.

Now It's Your Turn

What is it like in your culture? Are people relaxed during delays, or do they expect things to run on time? Do they become impatient if there are problems?

PRESENTATION EXERCISE

Plan a presentation on a topic of your choice.

If you are in a class
Write on pieces of paper the last-minute problems mentioned previously. Place them in a hat. When you get up to give your speech, draw out of the hat one of the pieces of paper. Take five minutes to plan the changes in your presentation. Write down the changes you come up with for later use. Give the modified presentation.

If you are working alone
Choose three last-minute problems and think about how the problems affect your presentation. What changes do you have to make? Take careful notes on your process.

OBSERVE AND GIVE FEEDBACK

As a class, role-play a meeting with your coworkers. Tell them about your presentation, what happened, and how you handled the last-minute problem. Use the information in your notes from the preceding exercise. Your coworkers, responding sympathetically to your plight, give you feedback and offer other suggestions for what else you might have done. Notice any differences in how you and your coworkers coped with the situation.

Chapter 13

Professional Image—Look It!

First impressions—made in the first few minutes of meeting or seeing someone for the first time—tend to be lasting impressions. From the very beginning, therefore, you want to come across as a professional, both in terms of how you look and how you act.

Professional behavior includes many things. A professional is competent, knowledgeable, and responsible, responds in an emotionally mature way, and can work under pressure. A professional is prepared, arrives on time, and responds to the needs of the audience and the situation. A professional speaks with confidence. A professional is appropriately dressed, neat, and clean. How do you translate those characteristics into actions? It varies with the culture you are in.

Humility. For instance, in the United States, it is important never to tell your audience that you don't really know very much about your subject. This gives the impression that you are not knowledgeable or competent. If you seem to be wasting everyone's time by making them listen to a poor presentation, your audience may also judge you to be irresponsible. In other cultures, however, such as Japan and Finland, an outward demonstration of humility is very important. In those countries, unless the people you are talking to have been very influenced by U.S. business practices, you might want to seem a little more self-effacing than would be appropriate for a U.S. audience.

Emotion. The amount of emotion you may appropriately express in a business situation also varies with the culture. If you are speaking to a group that considers it inappropriate to show strong emotions in public, such as an audience in Japan, the Scandinavian countries, or Britain, any such display will probably be interpreted as immature and unprofessional. In cultures that expect emotions to play a large part in one's perspective and argument, such as in Italy, Greece, and some South American countries, the right amount and right kind of emotional display will be considered acceptably professional.

Posture. Pay attention to your posture and body movements. Different cultures have different expectations, but good posture is always in fashion because it is essential to good health. In Europe and the United States, standing tall gives the impression of self-confidence and power; holding your head high gives the impression of being open and honest; being relaxed gives the impression that you are comfortable and in control. All of these are considered positive attributes. In contrast, slouching makes you look disrespectful, and leaning makes you look unprofessional.

It is also easier to breathe when you are standing up straight, which is essential for projecting your voice.

In general, do not sit on a table, unless you are trying to give an impression of informality. Do not swing your legs.

Attire. What is considered professional attire varies from culture to culture, so always ask before making a presentation. If you are unsure, it is better to be too formal than too informal in a business situation. Especially when you are making a presentation, wear what is considered appropriately formal attire (almost universally a suit) in the culture, business, and location where you are presenting. Different fields of business require different levels of formality. The banking industry, for instance, tends to be a conservative industry, and dark suits are common. Advertising, on the other hand, is a field where creativity is considered an essential element, so greater flair can and should be reflected in your clothes.

Dress in the best quality of clothes you can afford. Certain cultures, such as France and Italy, expect immaculate attire—shoes carefully shined, no wrinkles in your clothes, color coordination, and so forth.

WORD BANK

immaculate (adj.), immaculately (adv.)	absolutely clean, spotless; spotlessly
attire (n.), attired (adj.)	clothing; dressed
flair (n.)	a sense of what is stylish and striking
decor (n.)	the decorative scheme of a room or other interior area
universal (adj.), universally (adv.)	pervading the whole
self-effacement (n.), self-effacing (adj.)	minimizing one's actions, being modest; having the quality of keeping oneself in the background
to come across as (idiom)	to give the impression of being

Vocabulary Exercise—Matching Synonyms

Fill in the chart using the following list of words. You may use your thesaurus or dictionary.

ubiquitous   pristine   impeccable
unsullied   apparel   comprehensive
decoration   all-embracing   garments
retiring   unpretentious   interior design
embellishment   outfit   unassuming

Word	Synonym	Synonym	Synonym
decor			
immaculate			
attire			
universal			
self-effacing			

Check your answers on page 154.

<u>Think about It!</u>

Imagine you are waiting to hear a speaker from another country on a topic of vital interest to your business. Your company has paid a lot of money to bring this speaker in. The speaker, wearing blue jeans, is late, has misplaced her notes, speaks in a low voice that is hard to understand, and finishes in half the time allotted. Are you pleased with the presentation? What would a truly professional speaker have done?

CROSS-CULTURAL ISSUES

One of the difficulties of working in a culture different from the one you were raised in is that our cultural values are often at a subconscious level. That is, they are assumptions about which we never think. Furthermore, it seems universally true that people tend to be suspicious of cultural approaches different from their own, even to the point of automatically judging the other approach to be stupid, wrong, and, sometimes, immoral.

Therefore, one of the best ways to learn about other cultures is to learn about your own, to bring your values to a conscious level and try to understand why your culture does things a certain way and thinks highly of what it values.

The next step, of course, is to be open to the values and practices of a different culture.

Now It's Your Turn

Can you remember a time when you experienced culture shock? What was it about? How did you react? Do you have a different attitude now concerning that issue?

PRESENTATION EXERCISE

Your company is thinking about entering into a joint venture with two other companies, one in a European country and one in an east Asian country. You must present information about your company and your ideas about the joint venture to representatives from both of the other countries.

OBSERVE AND GIVE FEEDBACK

Watch your classmates' presentations, or another local presentation, or one on television. Use the Presentation Evaluation Form in appendix E (p. 147). Take notice of the professional image the speaker projects. If you are in a class, give the speaker feedback on his or her image. What might the speaker do to come across as more professional?

Chapter 14

Practice and Rehearsal (Bringing It All Together)

Practice makes perfect.
—English proverb

WORD BANK

stage fright (np.)   Break a leg! (idiom)   confidence (n.)
nervousness (n.)   polished (adj.)   dress rehearsal (np.)
spectacular (adj.)   impromptu (adj.)

Vocabulary Exercise—Definitions in Context

Try to guess the meanings of the words in italics based on their context within the following paragraph.

> The problem with *impromptu* speaking is that there is no time to practice. You have no chance to do a *dress rehearsal,* and it's easy to feel nervous. This *nervousness* can lead to a lack of *confidence* in yourself as a speaker. It is hard to give a *spectacular* speech when you don't have time to practice. But you can still give a *polished* performance by using your *stage fright* to gain energy for your speech. In this unit, you will get a chance to practice your speech and learn to lessen or use *stage fright.* Take every opportunity to rehearse your presentations. A by-product of this effort will be an improvement in your *impromptu* speeches. And don't forget to wish your classmates and fellow presenters good luck the way actors do: *"Break a leg!"*

Write your guesses in the answer blanks.

impromptu   _____

dress rehearsal   _____

nervousness   _____

confidence   _____

spectacular   _____

polished   _____

stage fright   _____

Break a leg!   _____

Check yourself. Select the word or phrase that best defines the vocabulary word given.

1. impromptu
   a. new
   b. unrehearsed
   c. late
   d. practiced

2. dress rehearsal
   a. sewing costumes
   b. to hear a second time
   c. dressing for success
   d. practicing in costume

3. nervousness
   a. having the jitters
   b. a strong nervous system
   c. to be brave
   d. calmness

4. confidence
   a. sharing
   b. uncertainty
   c. self-assurance
   d. loyalty with

5. spectacular
   a. dismal
   b. loud
   c. easily seen
   d. sensational

6. stage fright
   a. fear of changing
   b. clumsiness
   c. speaking with a strong accent
   d. fear of performing in public

7. polished
   a. smooth
   b. shiny
   c. elevated
   d. funny

Check your answers on page 154.

No matter how spectacular your introduction, visual aids, or research, you need to practice; otherwise, your presentation will not be as good as it might have been.

Many people are good impromptu speakers (see chap. 17, "Special Presenta-tion: Impromptu Speaking"). Most successful politicians can prepare for a speech in 10–15 minutes, but if you look back to their first public speeches, you will proba-bly see much less polished presentations. It takes years of practice to be able to give a good speech with little preparation. It takes time to develop technique (see chap. 10) and to gain confidence about your presentation skills.

Many people suffer from stage fright. The best way to get over stage fright is to rehearse your speech, using your notes and visual aids until you feel comfortable and confident. Many people find that, assuming they are well prepared, they can use stage fright to enhance their performance. If you feel confident about your pre-sentation, then the controlled nervousness over presenting it in public will give it the energy it needs to reach the audience.

Think of your presentation as a performance. Before a dramatic performance, the actors in a play rehearse many times, and before the opening night of the play, they dress in costume and perform the play on the completed set using props. This is called the *dress rehearsal*. The ideal is to practice in the room where you will be making the presentation, wearing the clothes you will be wearing during the pre-sentation. If this is not possible, try at least to visit the room you will be presenting in or get a copy of the floor plan. This way, you can simulate the actual conditions of the room at another location. Give yourself a dress rehearsal.

Note: In most cases, such an ideal opportunity to rehearse beforehand in the room will not exist. In that case, do as much practicing as you can and then be prepared to be flexible!

The following steps can help you feel more comfortable and confident before giving a presentation.

1.   Practice in front of a full-length mirror.

  *   Are you looking at your face (i.e., your audience) while you are talking, or are you looking down at your notes?

  *   Are you slouching?

  *   Are both of your feet a comfortable distance apart?

  *   Are your shoulders relaxed?

  *   Do you look comfortable?

  *   Are your gestures natural and purposeful?

2. Practice into a tape recorder and listen to the recording.

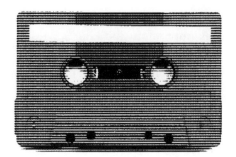

- Does your voice sound shaky or confident?

- Did you pause in the places you intended?

- Is your voice loud enough?

- Did you speak too low, too loud, too fast, too slow?

3. Practice in front of a friend or a video camera. Ask your friend about the following issues or view the videotape and answer the following questions.

- Do you look nervous or relaxed?

- Are you looking down at your notes, or only at one specific spot in the room, or all around at your audience?

- Does your voice sound confident?

- Are you doing anything that distracts from your speech (playing with your hair or your notes, rattling your keys, spinning your pen, etc.)?

- Is your posture erect yet comfortable?

4. Practice the last time in the room that you will be presenting in, if possible.

- Is there anything you need to change about your movements?

- Where will you place your visual aids?

- Did you practice looking at all of the audience?

- How are the acoustics of the room?

Tip about Acoustics

A roomful of people does not echo like an empty room does, because a full room absorbs sound more than an empty room does. When the room is full of people, you have to speak up more than when the room is empty.

PRESENTATION EXERCISE

A holiday is coming up—the one that celebrates love and romance (Valentine's Day in the United States, Lover's Day in Taiwan, Woman's Day in Kyrgyzstan—or whatever it is called in your country). You are the manager for the specialty gift shop section of the department store where you work. Prepare a special marketing campaign to get people into your shop to buy gifts (candy, flowers, lingerie, books of love poems, perfume, etc.) for the holiday. Think about things like special products, special prices, the decor of the shop area—and how you are going to beat your competition, the large department store across the street and several small specialty shops in the immediate area. You may also want to target a particular market. If so, how will you attract them? What advertising will you do?

You have to present your marketing campaign to the head of the store and members of the marketing department and persuade them to follow your plan. Your classmates will be the marketing department and head of the store. They will ask you questions, challenging your ideas and testing them to see whether they are promising and workable ideas.

Before your presentation, do a dress rehearsal in front of a friend, a coworker, or a mirror. Ideally, have yourself videotaped to see what kind of image you project.

OBSERVE AND GIVE FEEDBACK

Watch your classmates' presentations in your role as a member of the marketing department.

If you videotaped your presentation, use the rehearsal checklist to evaluate yourself. If you did not videotape your presentation, answer the first four questions, then have a friend, colleague, or classmate answer the last questions for you.

Rehearsal Checklist

__ I practiced in front of a mirror.
__ I practiced in front of a friend or videotaped my presentation.
__ I practiced in the clothes I plan to wear for the presentation.
__ I practiced with my visual aids.
__ I need to work on posture.
__ I need to work on eye contact.
__ I need to work on facial expression.
__ I need to work on pause and emphasis.
__ I need to stop fiddling with my _____.
__ I need to work on gestures.
__ I need to project my voice.
__ Other(s):

CROSS-CULTURAL ISSUES

Many cultures, down through the centuries, have taught the value of practicing.

> *First time raw, second time ripe.*
> —Chinese proverb

> *Even hard work grows easy to the practiced hand.*
> —Cato, 175 B.C.

> *Perfection is attained by slow degrees; it requires the hand of time.*
> —Voltaire (1694–1778)

> *Not knowledge, but practice.*
> —Greek proverb

> *If you have read over, you have still not read a second time, and if you have read a second time, you have not read a third.*
> —Talmud, Berakhot

> *Hand in use is father of lore.*
> —Scottish saying

Use maketh masterie.
    —Thomas Norton, 1477

Practice teaches us by experience.
    —Docuvius, 160 B.C.

It is difficult to retain the knowledge one has acquired without putting it in practice.
    —Pliny, A.D. 108

Suppose your wish is to excell
Before an expert practice well.
    —Chinese proverb collected in 1875

Practice is everything.
    —Greek proverb

Now It's Your Turn

What proverbs and sayings do you know that talk about practicing?

Chapter 15

Handling Questions

Asking and answering questions is one of the most natural things in the world, something everybody does. You've already asked and answered questions so many times that you may reasonably be considered to be an expert! Take that knowledge and apply it now in the presentation context.

In most presentation situations, you will have to answer questions from your audience. Decide whether you want to answer questions as you go along or wait until your talk is over. Usually, if the audience is large, it is better to wait until you have finished. Also, if there is the possibility of running out of time, you would be wise to hold questions until the end.

QUESTIONS KEEP YOUR AUDIENCE INVOLVED

Answering questions as you go along, on the other hand, can be a good way of keeping your audience involved. Moreover, give-and-take with your audience helps you determine whether they are understanding your presentation. Also, some people find it frustrating to sit in a presentation when they don't understand some part of it. Whatever you decide, let your audience know when they will be welcome to ask questions.

Almost always, you will know more about your subject than you have time to present. Your knowledge in reserve is the source of the answers to your audience's questions.

Anticipate Questions

One way to prepare for answering questions is to try to anticipate them. What questions do you think your audience is likely to ask? Another way to prepare for questions is to listen to the questions asked by your friends or classmates when you are practicing your presentation in front of them. What questions did they ask?

Were they unclear about any point? A third way to prepare for questions is to ask yourself what questions you had when you first heard about this topic. Write those questions down!

You might want to organize potential questions into categories and prepare for them, in case they get asked.

Sometimes a person will ask a question because he or she merely missed hearing the information. In that case, all you have to do is repeat what you have said—sometimes in the same words, sometimes in different words. Other times, a person doesn't understand the meaning of something you said, and you may need to explain it—give some background or implications, or tell an explanatory story, or give other further information to make the statement clear.

Repeat Questions

Unless you are in a small room where it is perfectly clear that everyone heard the question, or microphones are available to the audience, it is a good idea to repeat each question that is asked to make sure everyone heard. Sometimes you may need to clarify exactly what the person wants to know by asking him or her to repeat the question, by rephrasing the question, or by asking the person a question of your own. Then, answer the question in a complete sentence that gives the context of the question.

Difficult Questions

On the rare occasion, a person in the audience will ask difficult questions in an attempt to harass you. In that case, show that you understand and introduce an alternative view. Maintain your sense of humor. Different situations require different strategies: you may need to evade the problem by not accepting responsibility for the person's complaint; you may decide to evade by delaying answering the question; you may decide not to answer the question at all, and you are at liberty to say so, say why, and move on. Do not abdicate responsibility for the session to the troublemaker. Answer firmly and move on either to another person or your next point.

WORD BANK

to field a question (idiom)	to answer questions from the audience
to elaborate (on) (vp.)	to explain in more detail
to elucidate (v.)	to illuminate; to shed or throw light on; to make plain

amplification (n.)   expansion, enlargement, extension

ameliorative (adj.)   tending to produce improvement, making better

to amend (v.)   to remove errors or faults

refined (adj.)   purified, elegant; characterized by subtlety, exactness, precision

depiction (n.)   drawing, painting, sculpture; a description in words

to delineate (v.)   to trace the form or outline of

to portray (v.)   to make a picture or portrait of; to make a word picture of; to describe graphically

to illustrate (v.)   to make clear or easily understood by examples, comparisons, pictures, drawings, and so on

exemplification (n.)   showing or illustrating by example

Vocabulary Exercise 1—Expand Your Vocabulary

Turn the words in the Word Bank into their noun, verb, and adjective forms. Note that some words do not have all three forms.

Noun	Verb	Adjective
	to elaborate	
	to elucidate	
amplification		
		ameliorative
	to amend	
		refined
depiction		
	to delineate	
	to portray	
	to illustrate	
exemplification		

Check your answers on page 155.

Vocabulary Exercise 2—Definitions

Now, look the words up in a dictionary and read the complete definitions for all forms of all the words. How does the dictionary communicate what is a noun, or what is a verb, and so forth?

GOOD AND BAD EXAMPLES OF HANDLING QUESTIONS

Bad Example of Handling a Question

Q: I didn't understand your point about the new calendar making scheduling easier. Could you please elaborate on that?

A: As I said before, it will be easier to do the scheduling.

Explanation: The questioner wanted the presenter to give more detailed information and probably an explanation as well. The presenter merely repeated what he had said previously. Furthermore, the presenter used language that suggests impatience.

Good Example of Handling a Question

Q: You mentioned that we will be changing suppliers. Why is that necessary?

A: The justification for changing suppliers is threefold. We can get a better price on certain items with the new supplier, shipping arrangements will be their responsibility, and their computer system and ours are compatible, which will make the paperwork much easier.

Explanation: The presenter restated the question in the answer and then went on to give a complete, detailed answer.

CROSS-CULTURAL ISSUES

Some cultures think it is important to answer, "I don't know," if you cannot answer the question. In the United States or the United Kingdom, for instance, this is considered being honest, and it is believed that such honesty will lead to a situation in which the correct answer can be searched for and found. Often, the speaker will offer to find out the answer to the question or recommend a source that can answer the question, depending on what is suitable in that situation. In these cultures, any question is considered appropriate.

In other cultures, though, such as France, Mexico, and Japan, to admit ignorance of a topic, especially if you are either an expert or a person in authority, might cause a loss of face.

Now It's Your Turn

When is it acceptable to admit ignorance in your culture? Do you have to be careful about what questions you ask so as not to cause the speaker to lose face?

PRESENTATION EXERCISE

Your company wants to build a new store on the site of a park. As the company representative, you must describe your plan to the people who live in the neighborhood and answer their questions about the loss of their park.

Let the class members (or a friend, if you are using this book alone) role-play the parts of the people who live in the neighborhood. As part of their role, the class (or your friend) should come prepared to ask questions and listen carefully to what the presenter has to say. Let one of the "neighbors" be a troublemaker who harasses the speaker by asking embarrassing questions and making unreasonable demands.

OBSERVE AND GIVE FEEDBACK

After the presentation(s) and question-and-answer session(s) are over, discuss the following questions.

1. Were the questions fielded during the presentation or saved until the end? What was the presenter's reason for choosing one or the other approach?
2. Did the presenter repeat or restate questions so that the audience could hear them clearly and understand which questions were being answered?
3. Did the presenter anticipate the questions? That is, did the presenter seem prepared for the questions?
4. Did the presenter answer the questions patiently and politely?
5. Were the questions answered thoroughly, expertly, and to the satisfaction of the audience?

Chapter 16

Special Presentation 1: Introducing Others

Often, when a person gets up to make a presentation, someone else will introduce the speaker. If you are asked to introduce a speaker, what do you do?

Sometimes you will be asked to introduce someone you already know. If you do not already know the person, find out something about him or her. Interview the person, do research, ask others who know the speaker.

Depending on the circumstances (a company banquet or a conference session, for instance), your introduction may include information about the speaker's education or work background or personal information, for example, facts about the speaker's "family status" (married? children?) community work, and hobbies.

The introduction you make should be complimentary, usually with one or two humorous or endearing anecdotes and background information that indicates why the person is qualified to be the speaker of the occasion.

The goal is to warm the audience toward the speaker and help the speaker feel comfortable and welcome in your setting.

An introduction can begin in any way you want it to, but there are some set phrases that are often used at different stages of the introduction.

At any point in the introduction

We are honored that our illustrious speaker could join us today . . . (very formal)

We're glad (s)he could be here today . . . (informal to moderately formal)

At the end of your introduction

I'm pleased to be able to introduce to you speaker's name. (moderately formal to very formal)

It's a pleasure to introduce to you speaker's name. (moderately formal to very formal)

Please join me in welcoming speaker's name. (moderately formal to very formal)

What Your Dictionary May Not Tell You!

A note on meaning

To join in welcoming is a signal for the audience to applaud.

And, now, here's speaker's name. (somewhat informal)

Note: If the occasion is formal, you will probably use the speaker's full name and title; if it is informal, the first name may be sufficient. If you aren't sure, check with someone who can tell you.

PRESENTATION EXERCISES—FIND OUT ABOUT THE SPEAKER

Exercise 1

In pairs, interview your partner. Find out enough information to be able to introduce him or her to the class or to a third party. Try to make the introduction memorable, with stories or facts that others do not know about the person.

Exercise 2

Brainstorm about the kinds of information you could talk about when introducing someone under the following circumstances. Then role-play the introduction.

a. *A retirement banquet:* Introduce a person retiring after a long career.
b. *An annual retreat:* Introduce the inspirational speaker, a person from outside the company.
c. *A professional conference:* Introduce the keynote speaker.

Chapter 17

Special Presentation 2: Impromptu Speaking

Developing skill at impromptu speaking is essential for people who want to advance in their chosen careers. You will be constantly called upon to give impromptu speeches. At the retirement party of a colleague, at the annual holiday office party, during a toast at a meal, you may be called on to say "a few words." Or, you may be in a meeting where a question or issue comes up that you are asked to speak about, even though you hadn't prepared. How well you speak on these occasions can leave a lasting mark on the minds of your colleagues.

Tips for Successful Impromptu Speeches

1. Take a minute to decide on a main idea and the support for that idea.
2. Write these down on a piece of paper or a note card.
3. Concentrate on your technique—look confident!
4. Do not speak until you know what you are going to say!

PRESENTATION EXERCISES

Take the opportunity to practice impromptu speaking in impromptu exercise 1. Then discuss as a class, or with a colleague, what you could have done better. After you have had a chance to reflect on your first speech, go on to impromptu exercise 2. These topics are more realistic and closer to a situation you might find yourself in. Use what you learned in your first speech to help you improve your second.

Impromptu Exercise 1—Practice

Impromptu speaking is difficult because you don't know ahead of time what you will be speaking about and you have little time to prepare. In order to simulate this situation, write the topics that follow on pieces of paper and fold them so you can't read them. Put the pieces of paper in a hat or bowl or bag and draw a topic out. Take two minutes to prepare a speech on the topic.

Eating nutritious meals

Why (person of your choice) should be head of state of your country

Response to an award you have just won

Your hero or an important role model in your life

Your favorite actor or character in a book or person in history

Your country at the Olympics

Your classmates ask you to give a speech at a school reunion

Tell why the class or your friend should eat at your favorite restaurant

Describe a favorite vacation spot you have visited or would like to visit

After you finish your first speech, use this space to note areas where you can improve.

Impromptu Exercise 2—Real-Life Situations

After you have reflected on your impromptu speeches either individually or as a class, you are ready to do a real-life impromptu speech. As you did last time, put these topics on pieces of paper in a bag and draw out a topic. This time, take five minutes to prepare.

1. The president or leader of your country is about to make a speech. The person originally scheduled to introduce the president is too ill to do so. You have been asked to introduce the speaker to the audience.

2. It is your last day at work, and they are having a farewell party for you. You receive a parting gift, and the group asks you to make a speech.

3. You have just gotten a new job. It is your first day on the job, and you are attending your first meeting. Your boss asks you to tell your new colleagues about yourself and what you will bring to the company.

4. You are at your company's annual holiday party. You are surprised when the president of the company announces that you have been named Employee of the Year. Make an acceptance speech.

5. You are at a formal banquet given on behalf of your company's best clients. At the party, your boss tells you that she has lost her voice and asks you to give the toast before the meal.

6. You have just been promoted. The editor of your company newsletter calls to congratulate you and asks for a statement.

Look back at the suggestions you wrote for yourself after your first impromptu speech. Did you improve in the areas you wanted to?

Chapter 18

Special Presentation 3:
Dealing with the Media

The media and your performance on camera can do a lot to influence what the public thinks of you and your company.

TIPS FOR ON-CAMERA INTERVIEWS

In general, when you are being interviewed on camera, look at the interviewer, not the camera. However, if it is a formal interview or you are making a prepared statement for the public, look at the camera—you are establishing eye contact with your audience.

Don't wear either white or a busy pattern. Do not wear any noisy or dangly jewelry, especially if you are wearing a clip-on microphone. Check a mirror before you go on—look at your hair, your teeth, and your clothes.

During the interview, if you are sitting, unbutton your suit coat. Sit on the tail of your coat to keep it from riding up in back and scrunching up around your ears.

Avoid making an impromptu speech. A permanent record of your words is being made that will be broadcast before many thousands or millions of people.

Check the accuracy of everything you plan to say. Get the approval of your company higher-ups or anyone else whose approval is needed. Convey a positive image; use words that carry positive connotations, even if you are saying something negative.

You are on the media's turf—don't give them too much power over you. Ask for a list of the questions you will be asked. Negotiate, if you have to.

Learn to speak in sound bites. That is, remember that you don't have much time. Be very precise, very concise, and very succinct. Get right to the point; don't waste words; formulate your answer in memorable terms, if possible.

Most important of all, never make an enemy of the media.

PRESENTATION EXERCISES—DEALING WITH THE MEDIA

Exercise 1

Make a short statement to the press announcing a new product line or other expansion of your company.

Exercise 2

Role-play in pairs, one person being the interviewer and the other the interviewee. Then switch positions.

a. You are the CEO of a large automobile company. The media has reported that one of your cars tips over when going around curves at high speeds. You have to do damage control.

b. You are the human resources manager of a company that has just announced a move of its headquarters to another part of the country. The employees are welcome to make the move with the company. A newspaper reporter is coming to do an on-site interview with you about how the employees feel about the move, what they might gain, and what they might lose.

c. Your company is about to make severe cutbacks, including downsizing (laying off) 500 employees. You are the company spokesperson who has called a press conference to announce the cutbacks and layoffs.

Chapter 19

Special Presentation 4:
Hotel Project

This is an option for a longer-term presentation project. Depending on the learners' level of English and knowledge about business and the class size and length of time, this project can be expanded or shortened to fit the needs of each situation.

HOTEL PROJECT

In small groups, you will make plans to open a hotel. You will make decisions about what your hotel will be like, you will write a business plan and a marketing plan, and you will make a presentation about your hotel to funders, probably bankers.

Additional instructions: Use your imagination and have fun!

Where will your hotel be located?

What kinds of clientele (guests) will the hotel cater to?

Business travelers   Families
Singles   Sports groups

As a result of your decisions, what image should the hotel have?

Grand and luxurious
Good value for the money
Friendly and welcoming
Businesslike and efficient

What decor should your hotel have?

Modern and high-tech
Old-fashioned and comfortable
Exotic
Glamorous

The idea behind the hotel project comes from an exercise on pages 65–67 of *Business Objectives,* by Vickie Hollett (Oxford: Oxford University Press, 1991).

What facilities should the hotel have?

Gift shop   Hairdresser/salon
Conference facilities   Library
Dancing (type?)   Grounds/gardens
Park/playground for children
Gym: workout room; sauna; steam room
Sports: pool (indoor, outdoor); tennis courts; golf; skiing

What restaurants should the hotel have?

Coffee shop or tearoom
Snack bar by the pool
Fine dining: French, Chinese, seafood, local specialties

What services should the hotel provide?

24-hour reception desk   Child care/babysitting
Nightly shoe cleaning   Laundry; dry cleaning
Hourly bus/limousine service to airport
Office services—computers, printing, photocopying, faxing

What form of business ownership will this be?

Sole proprietorship   Partnership
Corporation   Joint venture
Other (different countries have different kinds of business ownership)

Financing

Write a business plan (see the Sample Business Plan on p. 132). Take into account the current economic environment and international implications.

Marketing

Using the four Ps (Product, Price, Place, Promotion), make marketing plans. How will you advertise?

Customer Service

What will you do to make sure your customers are happy and will recommend your hotel to others?

Management

Describe your training program for employees.
How will you motivate your employees to provide good service?

SAMPLE BUSINESS PLAN

This is a sample of a real business plan that a business in the United States might have to write for a bank or other funder. Decide which parts are relevant to the hotel business and skip the others.

Section I. Summary of Overall Plan [you have to wait until you are finished to be able to write the summary]

Section II. Business Description Segment
A.   General description of venture, product, or service
B.   Industry background
C.   Company history or background [since this isn't a real situation, you may either invent a company or skip this step]
D.   Goals/potential of the venture
E.   Uniqueness of product or service [since hotels are not unique—unless you locate your hotel in a place where there are no hotels already—what will make your hotel special, different, something that will attract customers?]

Section III. Marketing Segment
A.   Research and analysis
  1.   Target market (customers) [who will you cater to?]
  2.   Market size and trends [are there a lot of hotels now? will there be a lot of them soon? will the market change, say, become increasingly international?]
  3.   Competition [who's your competition? are they good?]
  4.   Estimated market share
B.   Marketing plan
  1.   Marketing strategy: sales and distribution
  2.   Pricing
  3.   Advertising and promotions

Section IV. Research, Design, and Development Segment
A.   Development and design plans
B.   Technical research results
C.   Research assistance needs
D.   Cost structure

Sample Business Plan is from Donald F. Kuratko and Richard M. Hodgetts, *Entrepreneurship: A Contemporary Approach,* 2d ed. (Hinsdale, Ill.: Dryden Press 1992), 234–35.

Section V. Manufacturing Segment
A.   Location analysis
B.   Production needs: facilities and equipment
C.   Suppliers' transportation factors
D.   Labor supply
E.   Manufacturing cost data

Section VI. Management Segment
A.   Management team: key personnel
B.   Legal structure: ownership; stock agreements; employee agreements, etc.
C.   Board of directors, advisors, consultants, etc.

Section VII. Critical Risks Segment
A.   Potential problems
B.   Obstacles and risks
C.   Alternative courses of action

Section VIII. Financial Segment
A.   Financial forecast
       1.   Profit and loss
       2.   Cash flow
       3.   Break-even analysis
       4.   Cost controls
B.   Sources and use of funds
C.   Budgeting plans
D.   Stages of financing

Section IX. Milestone Schedule Segment
A.   Timing and objectives
B.   Deadlines/milestones
C.   Relationship of events

Section X. Appendix and/or Bibliography

PRESENTATION!

This is your chance to convince your bankers that you have a great business idea, that you have the knowledge and skills to make it work, and that they ought to loan you lots of money! Good luck!

In your group, plan a group presentation in which each of you has to speak for part of the presentation time.

The audience of this presentation will be your classmates or colleagues playing the role of bankers and other funders. (When they make their presentations, you will be the bankers.) The purpose of your presentation is to convince them to fund your hotel project. Their role will be to question and challenge you to make sure you are a good investment.

Plan your presentation

Decide what information is essential to communicate to the funders.

Plan a convincing closing to your presentation.

Plan an impressive beginning to your presentation.

Organize the information in a way that is appropriate to your audience.

Language issues

Focus on language that you will need to use: vocabulary, persuasive strategies, and so on.

Practice key words and phrases, especially if you are having pronunciation difficulties with any of them.

Cultural issues

Take into consideration your audience's cultural values when planning your presentation.

Remember that you are selling your idea and yourself to your funders. They can turn you down!

Appendices

Appendix A

Some Information on Specific Cultures for Presenters

British. Maintain a polite, reserved distance between presenter and audience. Display technical competence to ensure credibility. Use humor but not at the start of the presentation. Avoid making a "power presentation"; convince, rather than overwhelm. Organization should be clearly segmented and follow logical (English) sequence. Use short case histories to illustrate important points. Demonstrate the practical use (applicability) of your information.

Chinese—Mainland. Show confidence (not humility). Persuade the audience of your honesty and that you truly have the money to do the proposed project. Use humor sparingly, if at all, and never use self-deprecating humor. Avoid making political references. Presentations are not used very much in mainland China, although that may be changing.

Chinese—Taiwan. Start with the largest concept, then move toward the smallest. A humble attitude is very important. Humor should be self-deprecating. Group-oriented persuasion tactics tend to be successful in Taiwan.

French. The French appreciate a presentation that is more formal than those that people in the United States or the United Kingdom prefer. Do not make a "power presentation"; convince rather than overwhelm. Clarity, subtlety, grace, and elegance are essential. Argue from general concepts or principles. Be very rational.

German. The Germans like a presentation that is more formal than the French presentation, which is more formal than those preferred in the United States or the United Kingdom. Avoid using humor. Impress your audience with expertise and thoroughness. Conciseness of expression is important. Organize the information in chronological order. Some Germans still begin a presentation by taking three steps forward and bowing their heads to the audience. Punctuality is absolutely essential.

Indonesian. Tell stories and anecdotes. Use humor. Grab their attention at the beginning. Emphasize the positive and downplay the negative. Be careful to cloak sensitive issues in gentle language. Stick to the agenda; follow it in order and keep to the schedule—especially if in a formal situation. Be gentle—never raise your voice in anger. Avoid discussion of religion. Stand still. Do not use too many gestures; an older, formal style used in Indonesia is to grasp the left hand with the right. In a formal situation, follow the cultural expectations of Peruvians (see the following); in an informal situation, follow the cultural expectations of the United States (see the following). Do not put your hands on your hips—this is considered a challenge.

Italian. Impeccable attire and manners are of the essence. Appeal to the leader in the audience. Express enthusiasm and emotion in voice, words, gestures, and movements. Do not be aggressive or argumentative. The poetry and music of language is appreciated. Be prepared to deviate from the outline of the presentation.

Japanese. Maintain a polite, reserved distance between presenter and audience. When referring to individuals, use titles and last names. Present to the audience as a group. Do not insist on interaction or eye contact. Be assertive but not aggressive. Be less animated than for an Italian or a U.S. audience. Work the parts of your presentation into a harmonious whole. Most Japanese people under the age of 40 will be accustomed to U. S.-style business presentations.

Malay. Malaysia has several cultural groups; determine whether you are speaking to Chinese, Indian, or Malay people. In general, British style is still practiced. Status, style, and formality are important. Follow protocol precisely, especially regarding titles. Show respect for leaders, regardless of their reputation. Avoid being cynical. Get locals to write your salutation—you must address the dignitaries with the correct titles and in the correct order of importance. After the salutation, spend some time thanking the audience, and especially the dignitaries, for finding the time to attend. Mention that it is good fortune for them to be there and a good omen for the business at hand. In your closing, spend time thanking your audience for listening and for being patient and attentive—give a gentle finale, not an abrupt closure. At the end, someone will often say a prayer in which it is wished that God will provide guidance to the business.

Peruvian. Wear formal attire and use very polite manners. Recognize the leader in the group or audience. Enthusiasm and emotional involvement are expected. Avoid criticism or confrontation; do not be aggressive. Be serious and professional but lighthearted (use jokes). Keep a positive, flexible attitude. Be friendly and conciliatory. Take your time; do not rush.

Romanian. Similar to Italian but more subdued.

Somali. Never use notes: a presenter who has to resort to notes is thought to be not worth listening to. Make eye contact. Use metaphors, stories, and proverbs to explain and persuade. Exaggeration is expected. Never joke about religion.

United States. A U.S. audience expects to be entertained: use humor and tell stories to illustrate points. Be animated: move around, use hand gestures, vary your facial expressions and tone of voice. Facts and figures (even projected figures) are considered hard evidence. Be future oriented. Repeat your points. Make the presentation as short as possible.

Appendix B

Additional Resources

Places to Contact to Find Local Speeches

Contact the rhetoric or English department of your local college, community groups in your area, and individuals within your company or organization.

National Speakers Association is *the* international association of paid professional speakers. They can be reached at

NSAMAIN@aol.com

Their website is at

http://www.nsaspeaker.org

and contains sample articles from the magazine *Professional Speaker,* a directory of speakers and information about national meetings.

Toastmasters, International, is the world's largest organization helping people improve public speaking skills. Their website is at

http://www.toastmasters.org

and lists contact information for every Toastmasters group in the world. In the United States, you can call them at 800-993-7732.

Some E-mail Sources for Business English for Specific Purposes

TESL-L, TESP-L. E-mail discussion groups for ESL/EFL teachers; TESP-L is a branch of TESL-L and focuses on English for Specific Purposes. Send message to:

listserv@cunyvm.cuny.edu

In the message, write:

SUB TESL-L yourfirstname yourlastname

(*Example:* SUB TESL-L John Smith). You will receive a welcome message that explains how it works and that gives other commands. There are also extensive archives of information available from TESL-L.

CETEFL-L. E-mail discussion group for ESL/EFL teachers in central and eastern Europe. Contact Rick Rosenberg and ask for help in joining. His e-mail address is:

rickpaul@ah.kiev.ua

Listerv@LATROBE.edu.au. E-mail discussion group for learners of business English as a second language. Contact Emily Lites for help in joining. Her e-mail address is:

lites@spot.colorado.edu

Additional Bibliography and References

Peoples, David. 1992. *Presentations Plus.* New York: John Wiley and Sons.

Shaw, Russel. 1996. "When the Presentation Went up in Smoke." *Sky,* November, 39–40, 42–43.

Snyder, Elayne. 1990. *Persuasive Business Speaking.* New York: AMACOM (American Management Association).

Information on Presentation Products and Equipment

Presentations magazine reviews presentations products monthly. For a free copy, call 800-707-7749 or 612-333-0471 and ask for circulation.

The following companies manufacture software, products and equipment for presentations.

Acer America, 800-239-2237 or 408-432-6200

ASK LCD, 800-275-5231 or 201-896-8888

Astound Inc., 800-982-9888 or 415-845-6200

Compaq, 800-345-1518 or 713-370-0670

Corel, 800-772-6735 or 613-728-8200

Epson, 800-442-1977 or 310-782-0770

Hitachi PC, 800-555-6820 or 408-321-5216

IBM, 800-426-2968 or 919-517-2430

In Focus Systems, 800-294-6400 or 503-685-8888

Microsoft, 800-426-9400 or 206-936-8661

NEC Technologies, 800-632-4636 or 630-775-7900

Panasonic, 800-524-0864 or 201-348-7620

Polaroid Corp., 800-343-5000 or 617-386-2000

Proxima Corp., 800-447-7692 or 619-457-5500

RCA (Thomson Consumer Electronics), 800-336-1900 or 317-587-4151

Sharp Electronics, 800-237-4277 or 201-529-8200

Software Publishing Corp., 800-336-8360 or 408-537-3000

Texas Instruments, 800-848-3927 or 817-771-5856

Toshiba, 800-999-4373 or 714-450-9150

Appendix C
Bibliography on Business and Culture

Beamer, Linda, and Iris Varner. 1995. *Intercultural Communication: The Global Workplace.* Chicago: Irwin Press.

Brislin, Richard W., Kenneth Cushner, Craig Cherrie, and Mahealani Yong. 1986. *Intercultural Interactions: A Practical Guide.* Newbury Park, Calif.: Sage Publications.

Brunner, James A., and Anthony C. Koh. 1988. "Negotiations in the People's Republic of China: An Empirical Survey of American and Chinese Negotiators' Perceptions and Practices." *Journal of Global Marketing* 2, no. 1. Also in *The Global Business: Four Key Marketing Strategies,* edited by Erdener Kaynak. Binghamton, N.Y.: International Business Press, imprint of Haworth Press, 1993.

Carroll, Raymonde. 1990. *Cultural Misunderstandings: The French-American Experience.* Trans. Carol Volk. Chicago: University of Chicago Press. Originally published 1988 in French as *Evidences Invisibles.*

Chu, Chin-Ning. 1991. *The Asian Mind Game, Unlocking the Hidden Agenda of the Asian Business Culture—A Westerner's Survival Manual.* New York: Rawson Associates.

Ferraro, Gary P. [1990] 1994. *The Cultural Dimension of International Business.* Englewood Cliffs, N. J.: Prentice-Hall.

Fisher, Glen. 1980. *International Negotiation, A Cross-Cultural Perspective.* Yarmouth, Maine: Intercultural Press.

Hampden-Turner, Charles, and Alfons Trompenaars. 1993. *The Seven Cultures of Capitalism: Value Systems for Creating Wealth in the United States, Japan, Germany, France, Britain, Sweden and the Netherlands.* New York: Doubleday.

Kaynak, Erdener, ed. 1993. *The Global Business: Four Key Marketing Strategies.* Binghamton, N. Y.: International Business Press, imprint of Haworth Press.

Kochman, Thomas. 1981. *Black and White Styles in Conflict.* Chicago: University of Chicago Press.

Miller, Laura. 1995. "Japanese and American Indirectness." *Journal of Asian Pacific Communication* 5/1, 2.

———. 1994. "Japanese and American Meetings and What Goes on before Them: A Case Study of Co-worker Misunderstanding." *Pragmatics* 4/2, 221–38.

Morrison, Terri, Wayne Conaway, and George Borden. 1994. *Kiss, Bow, or Shake Hands: How to Do Business in Sixty Countries.* Holbrook, Mass.: Bob Adams.

Rearwin, David. 1991. *The Asia Business Book.* Yarmouth, Maine: Intercultural Press.

Redding, S. Gordon. 1990. *The Spirit of Chinese Capitalism.* New York: Walter de Gruyter.

Scollon, Ron, and Suzanne Wong Scollon. 1995. *Intercultural Communication.* Oxford: Blackwell Publishers.

Trompenaars, Fons. [1993] 1994. *Riding the Waves of Culture: Understanding Diversity in Global Business.* Burr Ridge, Ill.: Irwin Professional Publishing.

Victor, David A. 1992. *International Business Communication.* New York: HarperCollins.

The Intercultural Press specializes in books in the field of intercultural communication. You may contact them at

Intercultural Press, Inc.
P.O. Box 700
Yarmouth, ME 04096
tel: 207-846-5168; fax: 207-846-5181
e-mail: interculturalpress@mcimail.com

Appendix D

Persuasion as Cross-Cultural Communication

Cultural values and assumptions play an essential role in persuasion. Here are just a few of the many topics that can vary from culture to culture and can influence how an audience will respond to a given proposal.

Harmony. In east Asian cultures, harmony within the group will often take precedence over other issues and values. If you argue for something that will contribute to harmony, you will be more successful than if your proposal causes discord. Discord within the group is tolerated more readily in European cultures and those of British heritage. However, like most cultural issues, this one can be thought of as on a continuum, and accepting disagreement within the group does not mean that people are not careful of other people's feelings. Saving face is important in all cultures.

Time. Cultures, such as Mexico, that are oriented toward the past tend to build their plans for the future on a solid past. Base your persuasive arguments either on a previous successful relationship with your company or on things that reinforce the audience's perception of their glorious past, the foundation on which everything today and tomorrow will be built. In the future-oriented United States, people tend to be persuaded by arguments that look to the future and promise improvement.

Rules. Some cultures, such as China and Korea, view rules as being less important than the context the rules were made for, believing that fairness comes by taking into account individual needs in a given situation. In "particularist" cultures such as these, people depend on relationships with other people to solve problems. People go to court only as an absolute last resort. "Universalist" cultures, such as the United States and the United Kingdom, tend to enforce rules and contracts more strictly, believing that fairness comes if rules are applied universally, regardless of the circumstances. A demonstration of flexibility and understanding will be persuasive in particularist cultures. A willingness to follow the rules will be persuasive in universalist cultures.

Leadership styles. Different cultures respect different qualities in their leaders. Some like leaders who are authoritarian (Indonesians, Mexicans); others like leaders who are solicitous and share in the decision making (Denmark, India). Some prefer a leader who is a generalist (Japan); others respect a leader who is a specialist (India). If you are in a leadership position, your ability to persuade your employees will be at least partially determined by their cultural preferences; and, to the extent that your presentation touches on issues of leadership and management, you need to be sensitive to your host culture's values.

Group. Group-oriented cultures, such as Japan and Indonesia, tend to be moved by arguments that benefit the whole group. Proposals that single out an individual for honor or that set up a competition among coworkers will not be successful; if proposals that stress individualism and competition are forced on people in these cultures, a serious problem with morale is likely to arise. In individual-oriented cultures, such as Britain or the Netherlands, setting up competition will usually be considered a good idea—the argument that this will be challenging and invigorating is readily accepted.

Status. Some cultures, such as Japan, France, and Mexico, grant status based on age, gender, or importance of family and professional connections. Other cultures, such as the United States, grant status based on achievement. When you are in one of these cultures, you need to have the qualities that are respected there in order to win your audience. If you are trying to persuade them to accept a person who doesn't have the qualities expected in that culture, your job will be difficult.

Religion. Never underestimate the role of religious values in decision making! It is never wise to try to convince someone to go against his or her religious beliefs, especially if they are strongly held beliefs. Make sure your presentation does not contain elements—either graphical, verbal, or conceptual—that offend your audience's religious values.

Appendix E

Presentation Evaluation Form

Presenter's name _____ Topic _____

Your name _____ Date _____

1. Content

   Introduction clear? _____

   Conclusion clear? _____

   Well organized? _____

   Transitions smooth? _____

   Signposting clear? (Could you easily follow where the ideas were going?)

   _____

   Ideas well supported? _____

   Topic interesting? _____

   Effective? (Were you convinced?) _____

2. Technique

   Good posture? _____

   Appropriate eye contact? _____

   Hesitation? _____

   Pauses? _____

   Voice loud enough? _____

   Speak slowly enough? _____

   Suitable facial expressions? _____

   Smile? _____

Gestures? _____

Movement? _____

Audience involvement? _____

Humor/stories? _____

3. Visual aids

Easy to understand? _____

Support the arguments/ideas? _____

One idea per visual aid? _____

Colors? _____

4. Discussion: Handle questions well? _____

5. What did you like most about this presentation?

_____

_____

6. What one thing could the speaker do differently next time to improve the presentation?

_____

_____

7. Other comments?

_____

_____

[This form may be reproduced.]

Answer Key

Chapter 2.   Evaluating Presentations and Giving Feedback

Vocabulary Exercise 1—Matching Synonyms (p. 8)

1. c, a response to someone's performance
2. b, to support a particular position or to disagree verbally
3. d, good; opposite of negative
4. f, to evaluate neutrally, mentioning both the positive and the negative
5. a, bad; opposite of positive
6. e, to express the negative aspects of something

Vocabulary Exercise 2—Using Words in Context (p. 8)

1. negative
2. positive
3. argument
4. feedback
5. critique
6. criticism

Chapter 3.   Planning the Presentation

Vocabulary Exercise 1—Definitions (p. 17)

1. to allot—to distribute, to assign as a portion
2. profound—deep, thorough, penetrating
3. appropriate—suitable, fit, proper
4. to fall through—to fail to come to completion
5. acoustics—the properties of a room or building that determine sound quality

Vocabulary Exercise 2—Matching Antonyms (p. 18)

1. to fall through—ant. a. succeed
2. appropriate—ant. d. objectionable
3. profound—ant. b. shallow
4. allotted—ant. c. not given

Grammar Exercise—Modals (p. 20)

1. I am supposed to write monthly reports for all the other departments. But, if I don't do it, nothing happens. (obligation without serious consequences)

2. I <u>have to</u> write these monthly reports for all the other departments, because, if I don't get them this information, we could lose a lot of money. (obligation with penalty)

3. She <u>must</u> have already left for lunch, because her office is empty and her coat is gone. (deduction)

4. This paper in the garbage <u>must</u> have gone through the shredder—it's in tiny pieces. (deduction)

5. My doctor told me I <u>have to</u> start working out regularly, or I could have a heart attack from the stress on my job. (natural limits; obligation with severe penalty)

6. I <u>have to</u> call my customer as soon as I can find a phone, or else I will lose that sale! (obligation with penalty)

7. I <u>should</u> call my customer and congratulate him on his daughter's graduation—just as a polite gesture. (moral obligation without serious consequences)

8. Thor <u>should</u> pick up the group at the airport because he knows the best route around the construction. (recommendation; deduction)

9. Thor <u>is supposed to</u> pick up the group at the airport—I heard Harry asking him. (expectation; from outside himself)

10. Thor <u>has to</u> pick up the group at the airport—no one else can drive! (natural limits)

11. The plane <u>should/was supposed to</u> have been here an hour ago, according to the schedule. (deduction; expectation)

12. We <u>should/need to/have to</u> order more memo stationery soon because we're getting low. (deduction; recommendation; or less urgent need; or natural limits)

Chapter 4.   Research

Exercise—Subjective versus Objective (p. 25)

1. Objective—backed up by scientific research
2. Subjective—a personal opinion without support
3. Objective—based on research reported in a reputable source
4. Subjective—a general statement not supported by evidence (Whenever you hear someone say, "everyone knows . . . ," it pays to be suspicious!)
5. Objective—expert opinion of those who base their statements on hard evidence

Chapter 5.   Brainstorming and Focusing

Vocabulary Review Exercise—Crossword Puzzle (p. 44)

Across

1. a specific, confined, limited topic (narrow topic)
3. proposition or conclusion to be defended (thesis)
5. the process of coming up with as many ideas as possible without stopping to judge them (brainstorming)

6. a critique or close study of something (analysis)
8. complete and authoritative; conclusive (definitive)
9. a general, extensive, large topic (broad topic)

Down

2. the goal, aim, target (objective)
4. to convince against, to deter, to talk out of (dissuade)
7. the subject, theme (topic)
10. to specify, clarify, to hone in on (to focus)

Chapter 6.   Types of Rhetoric—Persuading, Informing, Inspiring

Vocabulary Exercise 1—Matching Synonyms (p. 50)

1. c, reasonable; using rationality as opposed to emotions
2. a, the science of correct reasoning
3. b, disadvantages and advantages of something; for and against
4. i, to give supporting arguments
5. d, to claim; to assert
6. e, to finalize a business agreement
7. f, the science of persuasion
8. h, prevailing
9. g, to motivate someone

Vocabulary Exercise 2—Using the Words in Context (p. 50)

1. logical
2. pros and cons
3. reason
4. contend
5. rhetoric
6. close the deal
7. predominantly
8. inspire

Chapter 7.   Organizing Your Material, or How to Say What You Want to Say

Spelling Exercise—Hyphenation of Compound Adjectives (p. 58)

1. It was a well-known fact that the department head, though tough minded in business situations, volunteered time on his weekends to a youth organization, where he was known to be very soft hearted.
2. He was well known inside and outside of business as a person who cared about the community.

3. John Reynolds was the <u>best-paid</u> chief executive officer (CEO) in the company's history.
4. Of all the accountants, André was the <u>best paid</u>.
5. The merger proved to have been <u>ill advised</u>.
6. That <u>ill-advised</u> sales idea cost us over a month's revenues.

Organization Exercise (p. 60)

Setting: an informal, in-house meeting

 3 So, we've decided to go with CanTool. They are already tooled up to market in this area, with a solid distribution network all over Canada and in several European countries (U.K., France, Germany, Poland and the Czech Republic).

 1 As you know, although our company is only five years old, growth has been both strong and steady. As a result, we decided to look into a joint venture as a means of expansion. So, we looked into the possibility of working with a French company, a Canadian company, and a Romanian company.

 4 We're going into this big-time. We hope to have three new production plants going within six months. Charlie, that's your baby. Take anyone you want from Engineering to work on that. Your contact at CanTool is John Hastings. Susan, your department will be working with Larry McDougal. We want to have another two plants up and running by four months after the first three.

 2 Briefly, because of changing regulations in the E.U., we've decided to hold off on working with the French. Although we're keeping the door open for a possibility in the future. In the case of the Romanians, they are not yet up to ISO9000 standards. They'll let us know when they are—they're working on it, but we're not holding our breath.

 6 We expect to learn a lot from CanTool's experience in this area, and they're eager to work with us and expand on what they're doing. This is gonna be a lot of work, but we expect it all to be very much worth it. Any questions?

 5 And then, we'll be forming a joint marketing team with members from our marketing department and some of theirs. But we're relying heavily on their experience and expertise in this area. Distribution we're leaving entirely to them.

Chapter 8. Crafting and Using Your Notes

Vocabulary Exercise—Expand Your Vocabulary (p. 65)

Noun	Adjective	Adverb
spontaneity	spontaneous	spontaneously
	extemporaneous	extemporaneously
impromptu	impromptu	

Grammar Exercise 2–Combining Sentences Using Relative Clauses (p. 67)

1. I saw a stain on my tie <u>that/which</u> upset me.
2. The detective found the gun <u>that/which</u> was used to kill the victim.
3. Fred Miller is the executive <u>who</u> was promoted to vice president last year.
4. I thought a lot about the raise <u>that/which</u> I wasn't given.
5. The supervisor gave the worker <u>who/that</u> was consistently late a warning.
6. The president looked for the report <u>that/which</u> his secretary wrote.
7. He told the woman <u>who/that</u> you secretly gave a rose (to) all about you.
8. Greg knows about the woman <u>who/that</u> I hired for the job.
9. I followed the advice <u>that/which</u> my boss gave me.
10. I gave your colleague <u>who/that</u> you were telling me about an article on marketing in France.
11. Dick knew about the problem <u>that/which</u> his boss was talking about.
12. *The Intelligent Investor* must be the book <u>that/which</u> you were talking about.

Chapter 9.   Language

Grammar Exercise—Active and Passive Voice (p. 75)

1. I expect my employees to put in overtime.
2. My flower shop sells thirty dozen roses every day.
3. Our team decorated the banquet hall in the colors of the company logo.
4. Everyone receives a gold watch when they retire.
5. The company emphasizes honesty.

Chapter 10.   Technique

Vocabulary Exercise—Crossword Puzzle (p. 87)

Across

1. If a word is important in a speech, you should ___ it. (emphasize)
3. Use your ___, instead of your throat and lungs, to speak louder. (diaphragm)
5. Dangly earrings and shiny rings are ___ to an audience. (distracting)
8. The ___ in this chapter is technique. (emphasis)
9. In order to have good ___, you have to look at your entire audience. Don't just look at one person only or bury your eyes in your notes. (eye contact)
10. He didn't use ___. He kept his arms stiffly at his sides. (gestures)

Down

2. When you ___ your words, it is easier to understand. (articulate)
4. Don't ___ with your pen. When you move it around like that it's distracting. (fiddle)
6. His ___ was terrible. He shifted his weight from foot to foot. (posture)
7. ___ clothes are distracting. (trendy)

Chapter 11. Visual Aids

Vocabulary Exercise—Definitions (p. 90)

clutter (n.)	a pile of things lying in confusion; disarray
to clutter (v.)	to make a clutter; to fill or cover with clutter
right here (idiom)	in the immediate vicinity; this place
right now (idiom)	immediately (of time)
to gravitate (v.)	to tend to move toward
retention (n.)	the keeping of; holding; maintaining
to retain (v.)	to keep; hold, maintain
retainer fee (np.)	the amount paid to hire in advance the services of a lawyer

Chapter 12. Planning for Last-Minute Changes and Disasters

Vocabulary Exercise—Matching Synonyms and Antonyms (p. 103)

Word	Synonym	Antonym
flexible	pliable	rigid
backup	substitute	sole
panicky	hysterical	calm

Chapter 13. Professional Image—Look It!

Vocabulary Exercise—Matching Synonyms (p. 108)

Word	Synonym	Synonym	Synonym
decor	decoration	embellishment	interior design
immaculate	unsullied	pristine	impeccable
attire	apparel	outfit	garments
universal	ubiquitous	all-embracing	comprehensive
self-effacing	retiring	unpretentious	unassuming

Chapter 14. Practice and Rehearsal (Bringing It All Together)

Vocabulary Exercise—Definitions in Context (p. 111)

1. impromptu
   b. unrehearsed
2. dress rehearsal
   d. practicing in costume
3. nervousness
   a. having the jitters
4. confidence
   c. self-assurance

5. spectacular
   d. sensational
6. stage fright
   d. fear of performing in public
7. polished
   a. smooth

Chapter 15.   Handling Questions

Vocabulary Exercise 1—Expand Your Vocabulary (p. 120)

Noun	*Verb*	*Adjective*
elaboration	to elaborate	elaborative
elucidation	to elucidate	elucidative★
amplification	to amplify	amplificative★
amelioration	to ameliorate	ameliorative
amendment	to amend	amendatory★
refinement	to refine	refined
depiction	to depict	
delineation	to delineate	
portrayal	to portray	
illustration	to illustrate	illustrated, illustrative
exemplification	to exemplify	exemplifiable★
		exempificable★

★An asterisk indicates a rarely used form.